Out of Darkness

To Jim

A wonderful friend, great soldier and inspirational leader!

God Bless!

Luke Lloyd
22 Jan 2010
John 8:32

LUKE LLOYD

authorHOUSE®

AuthorHouse™
1663 Liberty Drive
Bloomington, IN 47403
www.authorhouse.com
Phone: 1-800-839-8640

First published by AuthorHouse   11/23/2009

ISBN: 978-1-4490-4767-2 (e)
ISBN: 978-1-4490-4765-8 (sc)
ISBN: 978-1-4490-4766-5 (hc)

Library of Congress Control Number: 2009911861

Printed in the United States of America
Bloomington, Indiana

This book is printed on acid-free paper.

To the Watchmen of Our Republic and Those Who Stand with Them

2. "Son of man, give your people this message: When I bring an army against a country, the people of that land choose a watchman. 3. When the watchman sees the enemy coming, he blows the alarm to warn the people. 4. Then if those who hear the alarm refuse to take action—well, it is their own fault if they die. 5. They heard the warning, but wouldn't listen, so the responsibility is theirs. If they had listened to the warning, they could have saved their lives. 6. But if the watchman sees the enemy coming and doesn't sound the alarm to warn the people, he is responsible for their deaths. They will die in their sins, but I will hold the watchman accountable."

Ezekiel 33:2–6 NKJV

Contents

CHAPTER 1

A Changed Man

Sam Flynn had spent the night at the Palm Beach Hotel, not far out of Limassol, Cyprus. The flight from the States had been uneventful, but his London stopover had cost him a suitcase, along with the frustrations that accompanied its loss. His destination was Beirut, Lebanon.

Over the years, he'd made a practice of breaking up long flights by stopping and grabbing a night's rest before reaching his final destination. Unfortunately, the events of the first leg of his trip and a restless night had left him tired and groggy as his alarm shattered a deep sleep and he shuffled to the bathroom.

His bald head betrayed his youth. A closer look at his lean, muscular body would alert any observer to the physical prowess of the man. Splashing water on his face didn't change his sense of weariness. It had been a rough couple of weeks in his Washington office, trying to keep everyone briefed on recent happenings in the Middle East; then, out of the blue came special orders for Lebanon. And of course, he'd been told he was the best man for the job. He had to agree. Experience was important. But the flip side of that was simply there were many men needing to acquire more experience, and they weren't going to get it behind a desk. Nobody really listened to his argument. They'd made up their minds.

Actually, he hadn't protested too much, even when his wife Trudy went ballistic. They had a wonderful relationship but the trip planned to see her aging mother appeared to be falling apart. At this point in her mother's life, delays always carried the old question as to whether or not Trudy would have a chance to see her again. So far, each of her setbacks had been overcome fairly quickly. However, all of her doctors remained noncommittal about any future incidents. Sam had consoled her as best he could under the circumstances. Finally, he'd said, "I don't think I'll be gone more than a week. Why don't you fly up now and I'll take some leave as soon as I get back and drive up to spend a few days with you both?"

This hadn't been the answer she wanted, but as a good army wife, she knew this was about all she was going to get right now. She'd fallen back on her old standby *chin high eyes dry* motto and said, "Sam, we'll make it work," just before he gave her a big hug and kiss.

Over the years, Trudy had come to learn the simple truth: Sam loved the opportunity of being in the field. Pushing paper was not for him. He'd grab any alternative that presented itself to avoid the mundane of the office. Most of his friends felt the same way. Being in the field always brought unexpected challenges, and he thrived on each one he encountered. His task this time seemed pretty simple. He was to make contact with an informant. Together they would travel to his home in civil war–torn south Lebanon using whatever transportation and infiltration techniques he thought were required. In the process, Sam would assess every aspect of his new friend's personality, character, and reliability while gathering as much firsthand information as he could about the sectarian violence. He'd done things like this on several other occasions. Such missions always came with a sense of adventure, and he was looking forward to every minute of his trip. He loved Lebanon and its people. He couldn't wait to enjoy the food.

After lunch, the flight to Beirut had been short and without incident. His reservation at the Hotel Phoenicia placed him in close proximity to good shopping, and he'd taken the time to pick up a couple pairs of trousers and some shirts before grabbing a nap.

He traveled as a businessman seeking items for his import-export business. Those who needed to know of his activities had been briefed. As usual, he made it a point to avoid contact with any U.S. government officials at this point in his mission. Such contacts had a way of raising the curiosity quotient among onlookers, and Sam wanted to avoid any suspicions as he began his mission. It just didn't make sense to do anything that could spark someone's curiosity about his activities. Rather, arrangements had been made to meet his contact, George Ayoub, at the hotel about eight that evening for supper.

Sam had seen a picture of George before leaving Washington, so they met as old friends and businessmen in the lobby before heading upstairs to the *Age d'Or* (Age of Gold) rooftop restaurant. He'd also read a file on George that led him to believe he could be trusted. From Sam's perspective, this was the most important information he'd acquired because they would be moving through dangerous contested areas getting to George's home tomorrow.

Sam found George to be very congenial. He had a good sense of humor, and they joked back and forth about their experiences in Beirut as students and Lebanese life in general. George took the opportunity to update Sam on happenings in the south while making certain he understood the dangers they'd be facing. Sam was well aware of his situation and evidenced more concern about George and his family than he did himself.

They'd both left the restaurant with a sense of reassurance about each other and the business at hand. They also perceived the beginning of a genuine friendship. As they parted, George agreed to pick Sam up about three the next afternoon for the trip south. It was hoped they would arrive in George's small village east of Sidon just before dusk. George wanted to avoid any curious onlookers who might spot a foreigner in his company and spread the word. He'd planned a supper meal and meeting with a group of fellow Christians who'd suffered at the hand of militant Muslims in the area like himself.

Most of the guests were already assembled when George and Sam arrived. After washing up, they all sat down together. None hesitated to talk freely about the mortar attacks and murders being committed by his Muslim neighbors from other villages. Sam understood their frustration and anger. He was certain he would have the same reaction if his family and friends came under such attacks.

With their meal over, other Christians straggled in to give Sam a firsthand account of the tragedies they'd experienced: being mortared, machine gunned, isolated in their homes for days without food, water, and medicine, as well as experiencing kidnap, rape, and murder of family members. He listened intently and responded sympathetically, even though he had no meaningful words of encouragement to offer. When things settled down a bit, George asked if he could lead the group in prayer for their friends and families. He no sooner began than a series of mortar rounds fell close to the house. Everyone sought shelter under whatever furniture they could find that looked like it would stop falling debris. Sam dove under a butcher-block table in the kitchen only to find George's son, Thomas, huddling there also.

Suddenly, there was an ear-shattering explosion as the roof over an attached bedroom took a direct hit and collapsed. Smoke and dust filled the air while debris of all sorts went flying everywhere. A scream let all know that someone had been hurt. Sam prayed to himself that these frantic screams came from fear and not severe wounds. Unhesitatingly, he and George both moved to the sounds and discovered George's daughter, five-year-old Hannah, clutching her thigh. A quick inspection revealed a lot of blood and a deep gash that would require stitches. George's wife had also gotten there quickly as a machine gun began to chatter close to the house. It was apparent the insurgents were nearby but no one could figure out what they were firing at. When it stopped, silence engulfed the house except for Hannah's subdued moans.

Without warning, the front door was kicked in and two insurgents jumped through it, brandishing their AK-47s at the group and shouting, "Are you ready to die for your Jesus?" These words instantaneously brought terror to everyone, and a mass exodus of many of George's friends ensued as they ran out the rear door of the house or jumped from windows while the terrorists' eyes adjusted to the light in the room.

Sam had remained cool. He hadn't known what to do. Being totally unarmed and surrounded, his first thought was that he would meet his maker very soon. On the other hand, he owed it to these people to be steadfast and strong in the face of danger.

Around him, a small group remained in prayer as they faced the dragon of death. Sam couldn't help but marvel at their composure. He knew they must be as fearful as he, but their fear did not show. In fact, they were calm and prepared for whatever was to happen. He was overwhelmed with the knowledge that these people knew their Lord and would go to their death for him without recanting their Christian confession. He'd never encountered Christians who actually faced imminent death but stood fast on their beliefs like these.

Sam was amazed at his own reaction. He had suddenly felt a sense pride and awe. He knew he was with them in spirit and would remain so no matter the consequences. As these thoughts sped through his mind, he stood transfixed, watching these two well-armed young men. They shut the door and moved menacingly closer to the small, terrified group. When they were within a few feet, they both lowered their weapons. The tallest one announced that they wanted to become Christians. Quickly, they said they had been reading the Bible and a Christian-focused magazine published in Arabic throughout the Middle East. One had been secretly dating a Lebanese Christian and was desperately in love, and both had the same dream in which they saw Jesus and were convinced to become Christians. They had acted the way they had upon finding the group because they only wanted to admit their desires to true Christians, not those who didn't have strong convictions and would run away. They knew, like Muslims, there were too many who talked about their faith but did not live it out. These people would compromise them, and they did not want them in the room when they confessed their desires.

Somehow, their leader had discovered Sam would be in this village and had sent a group of men to capture him. Fortunately, Ahmed and Ibrahim had been the two who discovered his presence. To demonstrate their trustworthiness and faith desires, they told Sam and George they could lead them out of the village safely if they would come immediately. They suspected a trap, but the situation was so volatile and dangerous both men didn't stop to think twice about accompanying them. The route was fraught with danger. They were fired on twice. During the second encounter, a bullet struck Ahmed in his right leg, and it was obvious he could not go on. Sam and George helped him back to the edge of the village to rejoin his group. When they had done all they could, they proceeded north and stopped along the coast to catch their breath and talk to Ibrahim.

Ibrahim was very worried about his brother. Sam and George comforted him the best they could. Over the next few days, Ibrahim learned through family connections that Ahmed was home recuperating and would totally recover the use of his leg. Ibrahim's disappearance had raised some questions but such things happened in the civil strife experienced in Lebanon in those days. Ahmed did not believe there would be any repercussions, and he let Ibrahim know it was okay to help the American.

The information gleaned from Ibrahim and Ahmed was invaluable. It brought fresh insight into the situation, and everyone was pleased with Sam's results. More importantly, Ahmed had agreed to provide information through Ibrahim and George in the coming months. In the process of all this, Sam and George had the opportunity to finally lead Ibrahim to Christ. Maria, Ahmed's sweetheart, had taught Ahmed about Christ, and he had accepted Christ's gift of salvation. However, both men elected to keep their new faith to themselves. Converting to Christianity could bring death not only to them but also their families at the hands of the jihadists during these volatile times. Both of them still had things they wanted to do to help stabilize life for their families and their community before announcing their conversions.

From this point on in his life, Sam was a changed man. It was as if he had stepped out of the darkness of apathy into the light of revelation. Trudy recognized the difference soon after his return home. Sam had not been hesitant about telling her of this special group of Lebanese Christians. In fact, he told everyone who'd listen. Their faith had been the final marker on his road to a personal relationship with the Lord. He wanted what they had, and as he and George led Ibrahim to Christ, he had sought and received the infilling of the Lord's spirit. With it had come a sense of peace and joy in his life, and this kept his walk sure and steady no matter what he encountered. It was exhilarating, and he now had the sense death was no longer an obstacle to his everyday living.

CHAPTER 2
Troubling Day

Rick Austin stayed fixated on the TV at his university office as a breaking news report and video clip of a plane flying into one of the New York City Twin Towers flashed across the screen. Then, incredibly, another plane hit the second tower, and shortly thereafter the buildings collapsed. It was an awful sight! Like so many, he was glued to the horror that unfolded before him. Everything seemed surreal; the airplanes hitting the buildings, people jumping to avoid being burned to death, the towers actually collapsing, ghost-like figures caked with dust emerging bewildered from the smoke, and confusion engulfing the target site while the newscasters speculated as to what was happening.

The thought of two airplanes striking the towers accidentally never entered Rick's mind. The probability of that happening in the United States just did not compute. As the stations began to replay their videos and repeat the events that had just transpired, Rick dialed his former neighbor and longtime friend, Sam Flynn, in Florida. He needed to talk with someone who might be more knowledgeable.

Sam and Trudy Flynn had settled in the Tampa Bay area of Florida following Sam's army career. Sam had been an army brat whose highly decorated father was stationed in a number of embassies in the Middle East. Growing up in these countries was adventuresome, educational, and totality absorbing for one of Sam's youth and spirit. He'd never given much thought to his semi-assimilation as he mastered the various cultural peculiarities of these countries. He had done it because he loved to play native and fool the local shopkeepers and others. In this process, he not only developed an affinity for the people and their traditions, but he also decided to attend college in Beirut, Lebanon.

There he polished his linguistic capabilities and mastered the political, economic, and social aspects of the region. His mom and dad had been happy with this decision because the universities there had great reputations; Lebanon was a stable Christian nation, and he would be close to them in Egypt. As his parents expected, Sam absorbed himself in his studies and his Lebanese friends while truly mastering everything he set out to do. The result was a highly polished and effective young man who, upon his return to the United States after graduation, acted more Lebanese than American.

Sam wanted to follow in his dad's footsteps and had enlisted in the army upon his return to the States. He gambled that with his background and hard work, Officer Candidate School (OCS) would be achievable. He wanted to be an officer. When he finished basic training, he volunteered for Airborne and Ranger training as well as a relatively new branch called Special Forces. Nothing excited his imagination more than being on the cutting edge of military operations. He sailed through all his training and was offered the opportunity to attend OCS, followed by an assignment to Fort Bragg, North Carolina, where he joined a Special Forces A Team.

During the second half of the sixties, he'd found himself in Vietnam twice, but the Arab-Israeli War of 1967 and its aftermath refocused attention on the Middle East. Following some schooling to check off career educational requirements, he and Trudy were assigned to the military attaché office in Amman, Jordan, where the experiences of his youth were utilized constantly. In fact, Trudy discovered an aspect of her husband she'd never seen previously and was as intrigued as the rest of the embassy staff. Sam moved with such effectiveness among the Jordanians and other Arab representatives assigned there, most people forgot he was an American. But the forerunner of Hamas, the Black September Movement, had begun to cause real problems in Jordan. King Hussein decided to destroy the Movement's effectiveness, and fighting ensued. One thing led to another, and Black September was forced out of Jordan. Their remnant moved north into Lebanon.

When he finished his tour in Jordan, Sam was assigned to the Defense Intelligence Agency (DIA) in Washington, where he traveled extensively in the Middle East on special missions. Intermittently, he rotated in and out of Special Forces units over the years. He and Rick had been together in Desert Storm, and Sam had been impressed with Rick's intelligence, dedication, and effectiveness in combat. Sam's last assignment had been to a joint headquarters in Tampa at MacDill Air Force Base, where he had continued his Middle Eastern travels. During this time, he and Trudy had several enjoyable encounters with Rick and his wife when Rick's active duty Reserve tours brought him to MacDill.

When his service ended, Sam elected to have a complete change of pace. Dealing with the nebulous intangibles encountered in the Middle East left him desirous of seeking practical tasks that were visible and lasting. Then, too, all those years of living and working in the area had not provided him with a sense he and his compatriots had accomplished much of anything. In truth, the Arab-Israeli situation was no closer to resolution than it had been when Israel declared its independence. Furthermore, he had come to the conclusion that few Americans knew anything, or cared to know anything, about the Arabs and Islam. In essence, the cold war had taken priority, with the result that our knowledge and emphasis toward understanding the Middle East seemed woefully inadequate and misdirected. Sam did not talk about it much, but Rick knew his feelings and stayed away from discussions involving the Middle East. If it hadn't been for Sam's attendance at retired officer luncheons at MacDill Air Force Base once a month and his participation in the Tampa Chapter of the Beirut Universities Alumni Group, Rick doubted that he would have had any connection with this region of the world.

In any case, Sam had turned to civilian adventures. His first was with an independent insurance agency. It was not a good fit and short lived. Relieved, he decided to find a different way to spend his retirement years. As it happened, he'd encountered an old friend who was now in the real estate business. His friend suggested that Sam might enjoy appraising commercial and residential real estate. After some thought, Sam went to school and was soon moving around the greater Tampa Bay area as a happy appraiser. He loved the flexibility and the interaction with many different people. There was no doubt in Rick's mind that the Flynns of Tampa were happy and fulfilled. Indeed, they loved the leisurely pace of the life they were living amongst their retired friends, and both seemed to relish their church and the congregation.

Rick's phone call that morning had found Sam in front of a TV at a local restaurant, where he'd gone to get a cup of coffee on the way to his office. Experiencing the same emotions and bafflement as his friend and those around him, he didn't have any answers when Rick had asked, "Sam, what's going on?"

He simply stated, "I don't know, Rick. We'll have to wait and see what the investigations reveal. Everyone's confused. Oh, my God! They just announced the Pentagon has been hit!"

"Yes, and we are getting reports here of a plane down in Pennsylvania. That makes four aircraft, Sam."

"I can't believe it. I never dreamed I'd be seeing something like this happening in our country."

"Me either, Sam."

Sam replied, "Rick, I've got to go. I've got to call Trudy." In parting, he added, "Everything smacks of a terrorist attack, but I have no idea where to pin the blame. We'll talk when things settle down. Take care!"

Sam knew it wouldn't be long before the truth was revealed. However, like many Americans, he was surprised that the participants were identified as members of Osama Bin Laden's Al-Qaeda group. Most Americans knew little about this organization. That wasn't true of those in government, who were aware of its existence and purpose. But knowing this while at the same time realizing the danger we could face were two different things. Most officials simply didn't believe there was a threat, or they scoffed at the notion that a group like Al-Qaeda had the wherewithal to engage in any terrorist operations against the American homeland. Of course, that led to a complete underestimation of the Al-Qaeda potential. In fact, even though Bin Laden and Al-Zawahiri laid out their rationale and plans quite clearly during the 1990s, only a few officials paid any significant heed to their warnings. The analysts simply failed to connect the dots highlighted by their threats and the overseas terror incidents that had been taking place since the 1980s. It was almost as if these overseas terrorist incidents against our citizens weren't considered serious or threatening enough to retaliate. Of course, once the cat was out of the bag, it did not take long for the fingers to start pointing. The intelligence community rightfully took the bloodiest hit, although the politicians were not without blame. The Clinton administration's opportunity to take Bin Laden out before he could create such trouble had been tabled, for reasons never fully explained to the American people.

President Bush's leadership was exemplary during and immediately after this crisis. He focused on memorializing the victims; calming and reassuring the nation; and letting the world know that the country could be counted on to initiate counteraction. Nobody doubted his resolve. Frankly, the nation was on the same sheet of music, and his doctrine of preemption seemed very appropriate under the circumstances. If "Tally Ho" had been the slogan of the day, most Americans would have responded joyfully.

CHAPTER 3
Rick Austin

As a journalist major with a minor in political science, Rick had elected to teach and do free-lance writing. His students were his main focus; he was never happier than in the classroom. He challenged them, just as they challenged him. His classes were always lively, interesting, and worth every credit hour. Over time, he developed a popularity that always insured a full classroom no matter when they were offered. His free-lancing provided needed funds for the family and exposed him to the practicalities of life and the world that enlivened his teaching. The combination made him an electrifying teacher, and he thrived on his work.

During his college years, he'd joined the Army's ROTC program and graduated as a second lieutenant. His political science studies and side interest in international relations made him a natural as an analyst in the intelligence community. But that wasn't adventuresome enough for Rick, so he volunteered for Airborne and Ranger training with a goal of becoming a Special Forces officer. Being young, energetic, and disciplined, he'd sailed through his courses without any major difficulty and had gone on to serve in Middle East-focused Special Forces units.

By the end of the first Gulf War, he'd risen to the rank of major, been decorated for valor, and decided to head back to civilian life. He'd been promoted to lieutenant colonel in the Reserves and was on the colonel's list for another advancement. His family consisted of his wife Ann, a son, and a daughter. His wife had never complained or indicated she was unsatisfied with their Army life. Nevertheless, he believed he needed to get back to the classroom. Additionally, he was convinced the kids needed a stable school environment.

With a significant number of years for retirement under his belt, he joined the Reserves and occupied an intelligence position in his unit. With so much going on in Afghanistan and Iraq these days, he did not think it would be long before he received orders to active duty. It was 2005 and he was sure Uncle Sam had kept him on the sidelines about as long as possible. Ann and the kids wouldn't like that at all. On the other hand, he might be able to get a staff job at MacDill. There were plenty of Reserve officers there, and although Colonel Sam wasn't able to offer any particular assignment insights, he knew Sam and Trudy would be thrilled to have his family in the area. Then, too, should he go overseas, Ann and the kids would have a great support team to help get through the tough times. For him, it was a win-win situation, and he made up his mind to try to swing an assignment to MacDill as his time got closer to call-up. Oh yes, talking to the personnel guys needed to begin soon. Greasing the skids would make it so much easier later, and he made up his mind to get the process started. But right now, he had another problem.

Ed Townsend, his editor, had called earlier in the day, asking about his next article for the magazine. Ed was a great guy and Rick thought the world of him, but he was awful pushy at times. Since 9/11, Rick had written several articles that Ed had been very pleased to print. All of them had something to do with the War on Terror and its impact on the United States. He'd started with a piece on George Bush and the direction he was leading the country. Next came some words on Donald Rumsfeld and the aftermath of the lightning successes our forces experienced in Afghanistan and Iraq. Rick didn't have many good thoughts about the size of the forces available for pacification nor their direction. To him, it seemed the inadequacies of planning for occupation and the discarding of the existing Iraqi governmental infrastructure and personnel had permitted the chaos and breakdown of control that ensued in the aftermath of victory. In fact, he'd been appalled at the seeming ineptness starting with Rumsfeld and his belief that technology was more of an answer than troops on the ground. You would have thought we hadn't learned anything in the previous wars. Of course, you had to be willing to accept those lessons.

His article on the Patriot Act and its contending factions drew praise from Ed but hostility from those convinced individual liberties took precedence over protective procedures needed by the nation in time of danger. He had anticipated such a reaction from individual rights groups but was convinced the current situation required stiff measures to enhance our security. He had reviewed the many restrictions put in place by President Roosevelt at the beginning of World War II and found they were severe; in fact, some seemed cruel. But they only lasted through the war years and served the country well. After the war, things returned to normal, and he expected the same to happen when the current fighting stopped.

To Rick, the situation discussed in the article was a no-brainer. He understood the issues were not black and white. Then and now, the lawyers and their clients constantly addressed every grey area they can as they fight through intricate legal points presented by either side. It is maddening. There are evil people who say they want to destroy the United States. He knew they will use every means at their disposal to do so. They have demonstrated their ability; thousands have died and are being killed daily. We need to do everything in our power to stop them. The critical point is coming to terms with the fact we are truly at war. Only those who do the fighting know the realities of the conflict. Those at home simply are not involved and do not seem to have any grave concerns about all the fuss. Rick was afraid it would take another 9/11 before the country really wakes up, and he shuddered each time this thought crossed his mind.

Everybody talked about Weapons of Mass Destruction (WMD) and the failures of our intelligence community to acquire accurate information. Ed asked Rick to tackle an article about this situation. Rick found that cutbacks in personnel resources, the reduction of human intelligence (HUMINT) asset efforts, the difficulties of acquiring and placing operatives in the Middle East countries, the inadequate linguistic assets for this region, and questionable information gathering priorities for the Middle East area all played a part in the shortcomings we experienced. Unfortunately, good men and women appeared to have been stifled by the system and the political games played in Washington. Rick tried not to lay blame while simply uncovering as many facts as he could. Ed liked the article, but Rick wasn't sure he'd been successful. Comments from various people made it seem as if readers often found credence for their personal views regardless of the position Rick took on WMD.

Then there were a series of short articles on the Guantanamo detainees, our inability to capture Bin Laden in Afghanistan, the instability of Iraq, the terrorist support generated by Iran, the general political picture in the region, Al-Qaeda and other terrorist organizations, the size of the active forces in comparison to it mission, the incredible impact of sustained operations on the U.S. military, the mess at Abu Ghraib and the damaging images it portrayed of U.S. interrogation techniques, terror financing, and the oil problem. Through their preparation, research, and writing, Rick had succeeded in reestablishing himself as a subject matter expert on the Middle East. What he accomplished would stand him in good stead if he was called up again, and he generally felt good about his work.

But one thing nagged at him more than any other. Just about everything he had written and read seemed to avoid any discussion of religion, or played it down to the extent that it didn't appear to be important to what was happening. Everyone in government and the media was focused on the political, economic, social, or military situation. In fact, since 9/11 President Bush had repeatedly told the American people Islam was a peaceful religion even though Muslims had attacked us and were fighting us around the world. That did not make sense to Rick. He knew it was good to be diplomatic in dealing with foreign countries, but something was amiss. It appeared to him that it was jeopardizing the things the country needed to be doing to subdue the enemy. This nagging sensation just wouldn't go away.

He knew one of the first principles of war was to know one's enemy, and that meant everything about him, particularly when a totally different culture was involved. Often, the most seemingly unimportant fact can have a huge bearing on decisions and their outcome. Rick also understood there were not many Americans who knew much of anything about the Arab world. Until quite recently, students of this area were few. The lack of interest rested with the region itself. Why? Because the perception was the Arab world lived in the past, not the present. Oil provided untold funds with which to buy everything and employ others to do the work. The individual economies were very fragile and didn't offer many opportunities for foreign investment. The political systems were rigid and highly controlled, and lacked many freedoms. More importantly, Arab society was encountering Muslim religious minorities desiring a return to fundamentalism. These groups wanted to go back to seventh-century Arabian governance and civil life. Their influence became stronger throughout the eighties and nineties and remains so today as they support jihadists.

He and Ed had discussed this dichotomy in the news many times. Their conclusion was that neither of them knew enough about the tenets of Islam to make meaningful judgments as to the correctness or incorrectness of any given article. This seemed to be the problem with both governmental employees and the average man on the street. That realization crystallized Rick's drive to do some further investigation. He had read enough to know that those in academia who were members of the Middle East Studies Association had let everyone down by becoming a "bastion of groupthink for scholar-activists peddling a politicized agenda that had become a … hive of academic opposition to America, Israel and, in a larger sense, rationalism itself … as professors continue to bully their students, apologize for jihadists, and teach fringe ideas in the classroom … while almost completely ignoring American national security issues and the study of terrorism."[1]

He was also aware that the government and its various agencies placed a lot of faith and trust in Muslims who told them about Islam. In fact, they went out of their way to hire such Muslims for advice and assistance in dealing with the War on Terror. While this appeared to be a bright idea, he still had some reservations about letting a foreign national tell you about his faith when you did not take the time to ascertain if he was telling the truth. Having watched Yasser Arafat tell one thing to the West and another to his people when he returned home had made Rick highly skeptical of putting too much trust in any Arab. Recently, he'd learned more about the use of deception [taqiyya] in Islam and was not happy watching Muslim leaders from various organizations move so freely among our unwarned and unsuspecting government officials.[2]

As Rick thought about these things, he remembered Sam and Trudy. They had set out to put their Middle East adventures behind them, but fate just didn't let that happen. There were two principal reasons. First, Sam always loved the military and he cherished the relationships he'd built up over the years. So it wasn't long before he was participating in several retired military veterans organizations. One of these was very active and held their monthly luncheons at the MacDill Air Force Base Officer's Club, where many of the speakers worked. Thus, he was being kept pretty well abreast of the Middle East situation regardless of his preferences. Second, the War on Terror was taking place in his old stomping grounds, and it was hard to block out media reports of current events when he and Trudy had been there not too long ago. So, he became a victim of his experiences and the real world around him.

Sam and Rick had talked regularly because Rick sought his wisdom in preparing articles for publication. Sam had welcomed these opportunities to share his thoughts with his young friend, and Rick always believed he was the benefactor as a result of their discussions. Also, Rick knew he was going to have to write an article on Islam and Christianity. While he had a good Christian foundation, it was obvious to him that Sam would be a great resource about Islam and any comparisons he might try to make in his article. Rick hoped to visit and have some discussions with them both. What Rick didn't know was that Trudy had led Sam in his development of a more meaningful and personal relationship with the Lord and that his relationship had crystallized one day on his mission to southern Lebanon.

As Sam began to grow in his faith, he and Trudy joined choir, taught Sunday School, helped lead worship services, and joined Christian organizations having an evangelical focus. Sometimes, the relationships encountered through all of these activities had left him with the feeling that some of his fellow Christians didn't have the depth of faith needed to withstand the challenge of the Muslims. He doubted they could remain in the room and stand with Christ, as the two Lebanese had. Not as dangerous but just as critical was his concern as to whether or not his brother Christians would be able to ward off the subtle and seemingly harmless initiatives being propagated by the Islamists in the United States and elsewhere.

Sam knew if we were going to know our enemy, we had to know ourselves to be able to stand against them. He was troubled by his perception that this staunchness of faith seemed to be missing in many of those he knew, and he feared they would collapse at the first true threat they encountered. He had witnessed this in the secular world over the last four years, and his intuition told him the same would be true when it came to those who professed a faith in Christ. That was not very comforting.

He'd come to this conclusion because of his perception that few people really had a personal and convicting presence of the Holy Spirit in their hearts and souls. The Bible was pretty clear. God only had one plan for each ministry of the church, and he desired that there be a unity of effort in achieving it. Ephesians didn't seem to leave any doubt about this. Yet, in situation after situation, there was bickering and infighting with few willing to give up their stance and idea as to what is right. It was almost as if they had been steeled against their fellow church members and the Lord. Breaking the deadlock often led to individuals or groups walking away in anger. To Sam, this meant that when the real tests came, as in Lebanon, Christians might scatter because they did not possess a bonded unity and faith in Christ that would allow them to withstand the jihadists.

In an attempt to assist in reestablishing a firmness of faith and sense of unity into the congregation, he had come to the conclusion that a comparison study of Christianity and Islam might be invaluable to his church as an evangelizing tool, particularly if he could emphasize Christian truths in the face of the Koran, Hadith, and Sira (i.e., the biography of Mohammad). He was convinced biblical ignorance led to every kind of manipulation, compromise, and pseudo Christianity. So with his pastor's permission and hours of study and research behind him, he taught his fellow members everything he could to help them understand the religious aspects of the two faiths, particularly their need to be strong and resolute in the Lord.

Meanwhile, Rick had been considering his own situation. Because of his experiences in Iraq and the research for his teaching and articles, Rick knew there was more to Islam than religion. He also knew that Sam and his friends in Tampa would be of great help in deciphering the Islamic doctrines he would need to understand fully before he wrote anything on Islam. Thus, he had tentatively made arrangements to spend a couple of days with Sam and Trudy in Tampa. All he needed to do was work out the details.

Rick picked up the phone and called Sam again. When Sam answered, Rick said, "Sam, it's Rick. I'd like to visit for a couple of days and pick your brain about the doctrines of Islam. I just think you and your friends could brief me quicker than my trying to read all the books I'd need. Is there any chance that I might fly down and spend some time with you?"

Sam asked him to hold the line and went to talk to Trudy. When he came back on, he said, "What about a week from Thursday? We are busy this weekend but if you came in on Thursday, we'd have Friday and Saturday to talk and you could be out of here on Sunday. This would also give me some time to see if a couple of my friends could be available."

"Sam, that would be great," exclaimed Rick. "I'll call later this week and let you know my flight arrival times."

"Okay, Rick."

"I am really looking forward to seeing both you and Trudy. Give her my love. Talk to you later. Good-bye."

CHAPTER 4
A Tight Circle

Rick flew to Tampa on the following Thursday. Sam and Trudy met him at the airport and took him to the Colonnade Restaurant on Bayshore Boulevard for supper before heading home. They knew he'd enjoy this, as they often met there in the past. It was catch-up time, and the conversation drifted from family and mutual friends to the various adventures they'd experienced since last meeting. Rick had that wonderful sense of family as they chatted back and forth. While he wanted to get on with the reason for his visit, the conversation put him in a reflective mood. He sat back and enjoyed the warmth and exhilaration of being with such wonderful people. Ann always told him he needed to take more time to "smell the roses" along the way and would be very pleased with his relaxation at this moment.

As they were finishing dessert, Rick said, "Sam, I had an interesting thing happen to me in the Atlanta airport today as I was changing flights. After walking around for a while, I went to the ticket counter to inquire about a delay in my flight to Tampa. Everything was on time, and I had about an hour before departure. I decided to wait in the departure lounge and make some notes on an article I am trying to finish for my editor. There was a brown envelope on the chair next to me. At first, I didn't give it any thought, as I figured someone was using it to save a seat. However, just before they called my flight, it caught my eye again. No one had claimed it. Thinking it might be important and left behind inadvertently, I did the Boy Scout thing and opened it to see if there was an address identifying the person to whom it belonged. There was no identifying information except for a torn, partial handwritten address in the sender's corner of the envelope and a recent postmark from Tampa. The contents caught my attention as they contained a document in typewritten Arabic. In these days, Arabic documents laying around in an airport make me suspicious, so I brought it with me thinking you or one of your friends might know someone who could translate it here in Tampa."

"That is unusual … I think I might have been as suspicious as you, Rick. I am glad you brought it along."

"I'll show it to you when we get home, Sam …"

"Let's wait til morning … it's probably just a mosque newsletter or some business document … we'll look at it then."

"Great!"

Sam paid the bill, and they headed to Sam and Trudy's. It wasn't particularly late but Rick could see that his hosts were tired. Nevertheless, they shared a nightcap. It was at this point Sam asked Rick to take a minute and revisit the reason for his visit. Rick told him about his various articles and the research he'd accomplished to prepare them. He said he began to notice that only a few of the articles he'd read indicated that the tenets of Islam were the root cause of the War on Terror. It seemed there were few authors who addressed the religious aspects of the current conflict. Everyone wanted to lay the blame on poverty, colonialism, totalitarian governments, unemployment, or some other secular, social, political, or economic cause. Worse yet, President Bush called Islam a peaceful religion and told everyone that we worshiped the same God. Rick said, "This just doesn't make sense to me. Our men and women are dying, fighting Muslims who use the Koran as their justification for attacking us, and our president says Islam is peaceful. I am not the smartest guy on the block, but something is wrong with this picture. The president calls for unity at the same time he fosters confusion and deception when talking to his people. They are upset with what is happening, yet his message does nothing to alleviate the problem. Sam, I know my perceptions may be way off base. I had to talk with someone about them, and with your background and friendship, I thought I could do so without repercussions."

"Well," Sam replied, "I hope you'll sleep better knowing I have had the same concerns over the past few months. President Bush and his advisors are making errors common to those trying to appease Islam without clearly defining their doctrinal worldview. They talk against the militants but not the political doctrine in Islam. Frankly, although it must be pleasing to the jihadists, I believe most Muslims would appreciate people who know their traditions, speak of them accurately, and do not minimize their significance."

"I am not sure about that, Rick. Based on the intimidation tactics displayed around the world and the closed minds you encounter when trying to discuss any aspects of Islam rationally, the truth may not be what is desired by Islamists ... that is, unless it is their truth."

"I understand," responded Rick, "but I am naïve enough to believe that we will never get anywhere unless both sides deal with the issues truthfully ... they just cannot be resolved any other way."

"You have a point, Rick, we have a lot to discuss. But before we get into our concerns about the administration and its direction relative to Islam, I thought it might be important to spend some time tomorrow listening to my Lebanese-American friend Ibrahim, better known as Abe since his conversion. You know I went to college in Beirut, Lebanon. What you probably do not know is a few years ago some of the various university graduates got together and formed a Beirut Universities Alumni Group here in Tampa. It's defunct now, but I joined. We had about thirty-six graduates from all over the state. Two of the members were people I worked with in the mid-seventies. I believe you know the story of my trip to southern Lebanon during the civil war and its effect on my life.

"My contact in that small village, George Ayoub, returned to his home when things settled down; however, he knew it was getting too dangerous for him to remain near the Sidon area. He had relatives in Beirut, and as soon as Hannah was ready to travel, the family headed north. As a university graduate in linguistics and political science, he got a job teaching Arabic to incoming Americans at the embassy. This all happened within six months of my departure. After twenty years of service, he decided he should bring his family to the States. They all wanted U.S. citizenship and were naturalized in 2001.

"We maintained contact over the years, so it was no surprise when he wound up in Tampa one day and called to let me know he was here with his wife, Najwa, and their beautiful daughter, Hannah, who had been wounded that night in south Lebanon. Hannah had lost her husband to unfriendly Muslims, but she and the children escaped. His son, Thomas, had become a citizen at the same time as his parents and subsequently graduated from law school. He joined the FBI and received training at Quantico, Virginia. Today, he is assigned to their office in Atlanta. Because of his embassy service and his naturalization, George was able to get a job as a translator for the FBI. His family settled into Tampa pretty quickly. Trudy and I have shared many pleasant hours with the family. Hannah's two children are terrific kids, American all the way."

"They sound like great people. I'll enjoy talking to all of them. There is simply too much I do not know or understand. Does George talk about your experiences together? I'd love to hear his take on your adventure in south Lebanon," Rick said with a grin.

"Don't worry, I am certain you will get the whole story from his perspective before you head home," Sam replied, without reacting to Rick's baiting.

Sam went on, "Coincidently, Ibrahim Schahab also moved to Tampa. You may recall that he was one of the brothers who led us out of the small village. After that event and his conversion, Abe accompanied us to Beirut, where he lived with relatives while attending the university. Because of the danger associated with his conversion and the fact he would be kicked out of the family once it was discovered, his change of heart was kept secret. Abe's political science studies opened his eyes to the real world around him, and his family's import-export business provided valuable insights into the happenings in neighboring countries. But like so many young men, his academic focus suffered a bit when he encountered Cynthia, a beautiful Lebanese-American girl at the college studying political science while reacquainting herself with her Lebanese heritage. It wasn't long before he was madly in love. He knew she felt the same way, but he had been raised a Muslim and unable to reveal his conversion to Christianity without fear of reprisal. Somehow, he made it through his senior year. In the meantime, his family had decided to expand their import-export business. They wanted to establish a connection in the United States, and after all the support they had provided Abe during his college years, it seemed only fitting he should be the one to go to America and set up a branch business. When he heard the news, he was ecstatic. There were no arguments. He left for Detroit within two months of his graduation. The problem was Cynthia was in Tampa and he'd made up his mind nothing was going to keep them apart. He headed south, set up business, and courted her. There was a problem, however. Her father put him through the 'faith grinder,' so to speak. As a Lebanese and member of the old school, this was very serious business to him. You know … was his conversion sincere or was he just saying he was a Christian to marry his beautiful daughter? Anyway, since Abe has studied and lived as a member of both faiths, I thought he might be one of the best to answer your questions, so I invited him to join us in the morning. By the way, he became a naturalized citizen in 1987.

"One more thing: Ahmed Schahab remained in south Lebanon for a couple of years. Like Ibrahim, he did not reveal his Christian faith to his family and friends. George and Ibrahim monitored his activities closely. I kept up with him through them. In 1980, he left the area and moved north. Subsequently, he immigrated to Frankfurt, Germany, where he also went into the family import-export business. Unfortunately, when Ahmed moved north, his relationship with Maria dissolved. As a Muslim, her father considered him a less-than-suitable husband. After all these years, he still loves her and has remained a bachelor. To his credit, he has been a truly significant intelligence asset in Germany. He has worked for our government, keeping tabs on the local mosques and using his import-export business to assist our agencies in the War on Terror. I have not seen him since Lebanon, but I understand that the business has prospered and he is getting ready to come to the States. I owe him a lot for saving my behind and being such an important and trustworthy information provider during those troubled times in Lebanon.

"I have to call it a night. Abe ought to be here about nine-thirty or ten. I just thought you ought to know a little of his background before we started talking in the morning. I had asked George to come, but he has some pressing work to accomplish and declined. Trudy asked

George and Najwa to join us for supper tomorrow evening. She said something about preparing a Lebanese supper; are you are game?"

"You betcha," replied Rick, "and I really am looking forward to picking your brains tomorrow."

With that, they both headed for bed.

CHAPTER 5

Getting Started

The next morning, Sam and Trudy were up at 6:00 am and off for a morning walk. They were sticklers about their exercise, and Rick joined them, knowing it would make him more alert as the morning wore on. After cleaning up, Trudy prepared a great breakfast. The conversation was light and enjoyable as they devoured it. When they finished, Sam told Rick to grab another cup of coffee and follow him to the study.

As they settled into their chairs, Sam said Abe would be along shortly. He wanted to gain a better understanding of Rick's knowledge of Islam and began asking him questions. Rick admitted he did not have a great depth of knowledge. He knew the Koran was the principal text and Mohammad had received the Koran as a divine revelation from the Angel Gabriel. He also acknowledged that when Andy Rooney had advised everyone to read the Koran, he had attempted to do so but found it was very difficult to follow and there were many conflicting statements that left him puzzled as to the accepted interpretation. He admitted he became one confused puppy by the time he put it down. He'd concluded although his heart was in the right place, he, like most

Americans, did not have a clue about Islam and how to uncover its secrets.

Sam laughed at his frustration and the truthfulness of Rick's observations. He indicated he'd had the same frustrations and gnawing concerns about Islam when he'd gotten started in his research. He too felt Mr. Rooney was off base because of all the books he'd ever read, the Koran was the least likely to be understood without someone to guide you through it. At this point, Sam decided to spend a minute on the reason for this.

In providing some basics, Sam offered, "When Mohammad first started his ministry, he lived in Mecca. His immediate goal was to win as many Jews and Christians to his new faith as he could. In reaching out to them, adopting many of their tenets. At this time in his ministry, he was very weak, and so the Meccan verses of the Koran represent a more peaceful and tolerant side of Islam. Unfortunately, thirteen years of preaching about Allah to the pagan Meccans, with their numerous idols in the Kaaba, resulted in less than 200 Islamic followers accompanying him to Medina. Once in Medina, history acknowledges his message was transformed from one of peace to one of violence, brutality, greed, and political power. This process led to the development of the Islamic principle of abrogation. In other words, while all the words of Allah are divine and worthy, those uttered in Medina are considered the best and abrogate or supersede those of Mecca. In a nutshell, this is the reason the Koran is so hard to understand."

Rick jumped in at this point, saying that he did not recall there being a Mecca and Medina section in the Koran.

"You're right, Rick," responded Sam. "When the Koran was put together, the larger chapters were placed in the front, whether they were from Mecca or Medina, and they were not identified by location of origin. As a consequence, there is no chronology in the Koran, and the reader must learn which chapters and verses take precedence through study. That is why you just can't pick up the Koran, read it, and understand its meaning.

"But that isn't all, Rick. Since Allah is divine, he cannot be wrong; therefore, the verses from Mecca and the verses from Medina are always true and correct. Thus, a Muslim can choose the verse he wants to emphasize and be correct in doing so when talking to an unsuspecting individual he is trying to sway one way or another. In the West, we talk about moderate and radical Muslims when we should be talking about Meccan and Medinan Muslims. I mean those who would emphasize the peaceful doctrines Mohammad laid down in Mecca as opposed to the more war-like and violent ones of Medina. These terms are far more descriptive to me, and they go along with the events in Mohammad's life that all Muslims must emulate to achieve a heavenly reward."[1]

At this point, Rick interrupted, "So the president is correct in saying that Islam is a peaceful religion."

"Only partially," responded Sam. "You see, in order to make this statement you have to disregard the preponderance of historic evidence along with much of the Medinan portion of the Koran. In doing this, you discard the most dangerous parts of Islam's doctrinal focus and mislead your audience. While nice to the ears, such approaches portend great trouble for our country as we accept them and relax our suspicions and defenses."

Sam went on, "That leads me to another point of great importance to all of us. Because we do not know the difference between a Meccan and Medinan Muslim, we in the West have adopted the terms 'moderate' and 'radical' to explain our enemy. But the fact of the matter is, we are not facing radicals. We have moderate Muslims following the Meccan portion of the Koran and moderate Muslims following the Medinan portion of the Koran. We do not have a distorted Islam. We simply have

Islam! I have often been upset by some of our speakers at the base who explain our enemy is following a distorted Islam. I know they are not being advised correctly and that their advisors should know better.

"Rick, do you have any idea why the so-called Western-identified Islamic moderates have not risen up against the so-called radicals?"

"It sounds to me as if they have no grounds upon which to do so if they desire to remain true Muslims."

"That's right, Rick. To walk in the Western way, they must become secularized and disregard the more militant portions of Allah's doctrine! The only time this has happened historically is when they have been militarily defeated and are weak. Of course, they can always play the secularized game while providing funds to support the Medinan Muslims in their fighting. That's what many have been doing and why our different agencies are taking action. Allah said if you can't fight in battle, do everything you can to undermine your enemy. Providing funds is specifically mentioned in the Koran as a way for a Muslim to join in the fight. Pretending to be a moderate while living in our society and providing funds for the jihadists is a deceptive tactic approved by Mohammad."

Just then, the doorbell rang. Sam said, "Abe might go over some of this with you again. We'll see how he addresses these issues." With that, Trudy went to the door and let him in; she offered him a cup of coffee before sending him to the study. As he walked through the door, he greeted Sam with "*Ahlan wa Shalan*" and gave him a big bear hug. Sam reciprocated and then introduced Rick, just as Trudy came through the door with a fresh pot of coffee and a cup for Abe. Trudy asked how Cynthia was doing. Abe replied, "She's doing well and looking forward to supper this evening. Can we bring anything?"

"No, Abe, I've got everything under control."

At this point, Sam chose to tell Abe about Rick's experience in Atlanta and the mysterious document he found at the airport. Abe's curiosity was raised and he asked if they had time to take a quick look at it. Both said, "Yes," and Rick went to his room to get it. Upon returning, he handed it to Abe and sat down to enjoy his coffee.

Abe opened the document and read several pages. When he finished, he asked Sam if he'd read it.

"No, I told Rick I'd wait for you to give it a crack this morning."

"Well, it's an old document, dated 22 May 1991. It was prepared for the Muslim Brotherhood in North America. It outlines the Brotherhood's strategy for subverting the government and replacing our constitution with Islamic law."

Reading from the document, Abe said, "Listen to this! Paragraph 4: Understanding the Role of the Muslim Brotherhood in North America: The process of settlement is a 'Civilization-Jihadist Process,' with all the word means. The *Ikhwan* [Brothers] must understand that their work in America is a kind of a grand jihad in eliminating and destroying the Western civilization from within and 'sabotaging' its miserable house by their hands and the hands of the believers so that it is eliminated and God's religion is made victorious over all other religions. Without this level of understanding, we are not up to this challenge and have not prepared ourselves for jihad yet. It is a Muslim's destiny to perform jihad and work wherever he is and wherever he lands until the final hour comes, and there is no escape from that destiny except for those who choose to slack. But would the slackers and the *mujahedeen* [fighters] be equal?"[2]

Everyone sat silently in deep thought. After a minute, Sam said, "It may be old but it sounds pretty significant to me."

Rick commented, "Whoever prepared this paper certainly didn't have our best interests at heart. I think we should get this to the FBI.

They might already be aware of this information since it is so dated, but it is apparent that someone or some group in our country is in the process of acting upon it or it would be in a trashcan somewhere."

Abe agreed, saying, "You certainly have a good point, Rick. I'd like to get this to George at his FBI office. I know it will upset our discussions if I take it to him right now, but I do think I should."

Sam said, "Wait a minute, maybe Trudy could run it in. Would that be possible, honey?"

Trudy thought for a second and said she had to do some last-minute shopping for that night's dinner and would be happy to do it if they bought her lunch later. There was no disagreement at that point. She took the envelope from Abe and said she would get it to George. With that, she was out the door and on her way.

CHAPTER 6
Down to Business

Having been a Muslim and now a Christian, Abe had a solid foundation upon which to base his discussions with Rick. As a consequence, Sam was a little surprised when Abe said, "George and I have been reading some new books that help clarify a lot of points about Islam that are confusing Westerners. The analytical approach set forth in this material is perhaps the most insightful and simple to comprehend we have ever come across in any of our studies. As a result, we will use these authors' line of reasoning. Everything they have written is based on Mohammad or the Koran. You can't go wrong sticking to these sources. Sam, if you haven't run across these texts, I am sure you're going to want to use this information in your own teaching."

"I thought I was going to be able to sit back and relax ... how can I do that if you keep throwing new stuff at me?" sighed Sam.

"You can't ... so sit up and take a few notes ... what is good for the goose is good for the gander ... remember? By the way, I doubt that many have run across this analysis even today. Let me assure you everything we'll be discussing is open-sourced. Hopefully, we will provide Rick with an understanding as to how one might counter the political correctness and the effects of multiculturalism in our society."

Sam blurted, "Yeah! These concepts have taken a heavy toll concerning the truth on our ability to educate our people about Islamic realities and the dangers around us."

"Before I utter another word," Abe said, "I want to make sure you understand not all Muslims fit the militant jihadist mode. On the other hand, I'm afraid the *unstated implication* of such a statement leads many people to the conclusion that the religion is not the problem. They reason, if it were, the entire Muslim world would be in this conflict on the battlefield."

"I get your point," commented Rick, "but there are many different ways to fight and support one's friends without being on the battlefield."

"Agreed, and we can get into that later. Right now, I just want to make sure we can all agree not all Muslims fit the terrorist mold. On the other hand, when I get finished, I hope you'll both agree the Islamic religion is a major source of the problems we face around the world today. Let me be very clear about this. To me, it is the central issue, and one that government officials and all of us tend to side-step, prolonging the day when resolution might be obtained. The key ingredient to overcoming Islamist intentions is education."

"Rick, I think it is great that you are investigating these issues." Abe added.

Rick responded, "I've always been taught to seek the truth, for it alone can set me free."

Abe said, "I wish more people lived by that principle … with that in mind, Rick, what is Islam to you?"

Rick answered, "A religion for over a billion people on this planet."

"Right, you've answered the question like the majority of people to whom this question is posed, and you are partially correct. Unfortunately, your answer totally overlooks the most critical parts of Islam. You see, Islam is a combined political system, culture, and religion all mixed together."

Rick mused, "I'll be honest, I never thought of Islam in this way. It has just been a religion to me."

"Well, I understand," said Abe. "Unless you have studied religions in some depth, you probably wouldn't consider it otherwise."

"I would suppose most people are in the same boat as I," Rick mused. "From what I've read, it seems a number of our academicians have made it a point to camouflage or even stay clear of the truth about Islam in their teaching. In fact, I've heard that noted scholars have played the apologist role for Islam. I guess everything is subject to interpretation, even a rewriting of history. I still believe their arguments will dissolve as more and more people uncover the truth."

Abe responded, "You must remember that there is only one doctrine in Islam. The newspaper writers and various commentators talk in terms of moderates and fundamentalists. But today, I know of no place where I can turn to find a recorded moderate Muslim-type doctrine that gives me the ability to intelligently support an alternative approach to this faith. There are many books with interpretations of what a moderate doctrine could be, but I know of none leading to an agreement acceptable to all moderates. At the same time, I know of no unified effort on the part of moderates to counter the fundamentalists and jihadists in a significant and meaningful manner. Some believe reform, or the development of a secularized alternate to current Islamic doctrine, is the way to go, but please understand that you would not have a true version of Islam or the Koran if this came about. It would be Islam in name only."

Sam interrupted, "Abe, do you really see this as a possibility? I am not sure I do."

"Sam, you're right. It is more likely that a tacit agreement can be established between the sympathizers of the Meccan and Medinan doctrines downplaying, or totally setting aside, the violent and war-like verses of the Koran in the interest of a stable and peaceful society. We experienced something like this following the end of World War II and the rise of the Medinan jihadists of today. Remember, it took physical force and occupation to set up those nonconflict years. Frankly, unless the Muslim governments get involved to stop jihadist activities, I am not sure I see much hope."

"Sorry, Abe, I didn't mean to interrupt but I just had to ask your thoughts on this."

"That's okay, Sam, I don't want this to be a lecture but I do want to emphasize the significance of Islam's being a fully developed political system and the oldest form of politics active in the world today. This is critical to our understanding of the Islamic faith. More importantly, because the Muslims do not separate the political from the religious, we grant the Islamist greater tolerance than we should. We talk and think about Islam as a religion, they talk religion and think of Islam's political implications for our country."

"How so?" replied Sam.

"Westerners have been taught not to criticize other religions," Abe said. "Political correctness and multiculturalism teach us all religions are equal in our society. These concepts are deeply engrained in all of us. Even our government officials are hesitant to bring up religion as being a problem. In truth, this blinds us to the dangers Islam portends for our country. That's why the truth about Islam is so important. It permits us to separate the politics from the religious parts and deal with them intelligently. Once everyone is aware, the battlefield changes and we will be able to successfully challenge those who are against us."

"Wow!" exclaimed Rick. "I never thought about it this way!"

"You aren't alone ... you have to understand, it is the politics of Islam that sets forth the treatment of Muslims and, more to the point, nonbelievers ... you and I ... as well. When you add to this Allah's political doctrine as being sacred, perfect, eternal, and universal, all other governments fall short in Muslim eyes.[1] Thus, Islamic law must prevail, and Islam seeks to establish a theocratic government to rule the citizens of any non-Muslim country."

Rick chimed in, "That philosophy is contrary to one of our most basic beliefs, i.e., the separation of church and state. It seems to me Muslims have a terrible dilemma. If they accept constitutional law and democracy, they must put aside the teachings of Allah and Mohammad concerning the establishment of theocratic governments."

"Yes," Abe said, "and that is another critical issue for all Muslim immigrants coming to our country. If they pledge allegiance to the United States and become citizens, they must lay aside fundamental Islamic doctrine or apply the Koranic doctrine of deception, meaning they work behind our backs to do as the Koran says. I do not envy them this quandary, but I do know there is flexibility within the Muslim world. History and the Islamic civilization have demonstrated Islam's ability to co-exist in the past during times of Islamic weakness but not during times of economic, political, and military strength. Turkey is a good example of the way in which the jihad doctrines of Islam can be suppressed, allowing its citizens the freedom of existing in a secular society. Even so, it too is under attack by jihadists within and without the country today."

"Boy," observed Rick, "that presents a heck of a quandary for our government, doesn't it? We all want an effective immigration policy, but how do you separate the jihadist and the non-jihadist? Obviously, we don't want any bad apples."

Sam nodded his head and said, "The Homeland Security and the Immigration boys have a big uncertainty on their plate. It is greatly complicated by those Muslims and their supporters who cry persecution, profiling, and equal rights at every turn. I know there are ways to identify these people, but I am not sure our agencies have solved this problem. Until they do, those bad apples you mentioned, Rick, will not be stopped from making a home here. The female *abaya* and *hijab* may be an indicator, but it is hard to know what's in the heart without an extensive examination by a well-trained individual. Even then, questions may remain."

Sam continued, "Both Abe and I want to make certain you understand it is the politics of Islam that has driven Islam's past successes. The record shows, as a spiritual leader in his first years, Mohammad only won a moderate number of individuals to his new faith. As a political leader and warrior in Medina, Islam literally spread like wildfire and Mohammad attained kingly leadership status.[2] That's why we need to let people know the difference between the religion and the politics of the faith."

Abe didn't hesitate, picking up where he left off, and started by saying, "Islam is also a culture that dominates one's entire life through its complete legal code called the Shari'a. It basically organizes the details and experiences of Mohammad's life into law. Those laws have become the responsibility of all Muslims to follow. That is the practical reality surrounding Islamic worship. However, the focus on Mohammad takes the spotlight off Allah, so I do not believe any Muslim worth his salt would agree with me. You wouldn't be a good Muslim under those circumstances. From my perspective, I see Islam as being not so much the worship of Allah as it is the worship of Allah by imitating Mohammad."[3]

Rick said he hadn't heard that expressed recently and was surprised it wasn't common knowledge in the West. After all, Winston Churchill and many others had called Islam "Mohammadism" for many years. There had to be some justification back in those days.

Sam smiled knowingly and said, "Yes, but as you know, the media can gloss over a lot of sticky subjects if they choose to do so. Of course, it takes a lot of time and effort to deal with the truth when religion isn't a big news item. Isn't the journalist's motto, '*If it bleeds, it leads*'?" Rick simply nodded.

"Rick, to me the religious part of Islam is very simple," offered Abe. "Essentially, it boils down to the five pillars and what a Muslim must do to go to heaven ('paradise,' in the Koran) and avoid Hell. I am sure you have heard of the five pillars before, i.e., the Shahada, or declaring that there is no God but Allah, and Mohammad is his Prophet; Salat, or prayer; Sawm, or fasting during Ramadan; Hajj, or pilgrimage to Mecca to cleanse away sin; and Zakat, or almsgiving to the poor. None of these particular features of Islam are troubling in any way to our tolerant society. On the other hand, the politics of Islam affects every Muslim and non-Muslim."

With that, Sam said he needed more coffee. Rick grinned enthusiastically and headed to the kitchen. Sam called after him, "How about fifteen minutes?" He turned to Abe and said, "This is great. I really want Rick to gain the knowledge he needs to be effective in discussing Islam."

Abe replied, "He should be okay when we finish," and the two of them headed into the kitchen, where they joined Rick and Trudy, who'd just returned from her trip to George's office. After agreeing on lunch in an hour and filling their coffee cups, the three men headed back to the study. Rick grabbed his notes and settled in his chair.

CHAPTER 7
Abe's Key Insights

As they settled in again, Sam told Rick, "I hope you are getting the picture that it is the politics of Islam that is so troubling to both Abe and me. We believe it is the most dangerous aspect of what Islam seeks to accomplish because it is hidden under a 'religious veil' and is not obvious to the casual observer. To us, it just doesn't seem prudent for our country to continue to look at Islam from a purely religious perspective. Somehow, we must break out of our strictly religious orientation and begin to be more circumspect as to the meaning of the camouflaged political agenda that comes with it."

"It makes sense to me," responded Rick. "By doing so, we not only clarify our understanding of the true problem faced by Muslims everywhere, but we also come to a deeper understanding of Islamists and the way we should be countering their activities. The old rules of treating Islam strictly as a religion simply do not seem to apply. It is easier to stand against militant jihadists on the battlefield, because they will fight openly. As you have pointed out, the dilemma rests with the sympathizers and traditionalists who are driven by their religious doctrines to nod behind our backs and stand aside as the jihadists exact their toll on us. Indeed, there are those who express verbal condolences while withholding any condemnation of their fellow Muslims."

"Yes," injected Sam, "I think we can all agree. The bottom line is simply we must be careful in our quest for freedom of religion, multiculturalism, political correctness, and tolerance in this country, that we do not turn a blind eye to those beliefs and practices jeopardizing the very things we hold dear. It may be politically correct to focus on the peaceful aspects of Islam, but that is not where our enemies focus. Remember, there are some who say we are not at war with Islam, but Islamists are certainly at war with us. Every day, we read about envy in their hearts and vitriolic messages against the infidel spewing from their lips throughout the world. Jihadists teach their fellow Muslims to hate, die, and kill under the banner of Islam, so they might receive a heavenly martyr's reward. There is no question, for most in the Middle East and elsewhere, these are powerful messages. They have won many converts to the cause. And to our chagrin, even those who have experienced the freedoms of the United States have rejected what we have and turned our openness against us. Particularly troubling is the fact many are educated, from well-to-do families, and have studied and lived in our communities for a number of years."

Abe then apologized to Rick for getting ahead of himself again. He said, "Rick, I am not a teacher. I tend to jumble things up or get ahead of myself because each topic is so important and interesting at the same time. Sometimes, I think I act more like a preacher. Anyway, I'd like to shift gears and talk about the Islamic texts and where one might have to turn to learn about this faith.

Rick murmured, "The Koran."

Abe smiled and nodded, "Yes, that is exactly what most Americans would say, because it is the most well-known source; however, the truth is that the Koran only constitutes one third of the texts needed to comprehend Islamic doctrines. Some have referred to these three texts as the 'Trilogy of Islam.'"[1]

"I've never heard that expression. I suppose it's only the stalwarts of academia who have tackled these texts and derived anything from them. In fact, it would seem to me most of the information and discussions would stay in lofty realms. Having said this, I guess that is one of the problems we face today. The information hasn't been simplified and made available to the public," mused Rick.

"Hopefully, you'll help us resolve some of these public knowledge issues in your articles, Rick," Sam offered with a wink.

Abe went on, "Without going into a lot of detail, the trilogy not only includes the Koran but also the Sira, or biography of Mohammad, and the Hadith, more commonly known as the 'traditions' of Mohammad. These three texts constitute the formulation and totality of Islam and must be taken as a whole, with emphasis on the unity of the texts when discussing Islam. Furthermore, every book of the Trilogy is both religious and political and very clear about the doctrine of Islam."[2]

Abe asked Rick, "Do you have any idea what it is that makes Islam so hard for Westerners to comprehend aside from the language, the scholarly approach taken by academia, and the fact that there are three texts needed to comprehend Islam?"

Rick said, "I'm not trying to be smart, but it would seem to me you have already answered your question. One thing is absolutely certain, I do not know enough about Islam to give you another answer at this point."

Abe smiled and said, "The simple answer is that Islam is a profoundly dualistic faith! Coming to terms with this fact is critical because dualism is the foundation and key to understanding Islam and to deciphering the aspects of it that confuse Westerners most."

"What is a dualistic faith? I have never heard the term used in relation to religion! Shows you the limits of my learning," remarked Rick.

"Don't be too hard on yourself," replied Abe in recognizing Rick's bewilderment and Sam's raised eyebrows. "I would guess that most, if not all, of your fellow countrymen are in the same boat. None of us think in such terms. That is part, if not all, of the problem."

"Okay, so what are we talking about?"

"Let me illustrate," explained Abe. "The verse, 'There is no god but Allah and Mohammad is his final prophet,' is repeated in one form or another more than thirty times throughout the Koran. Here we have the authorizer (Allah) and the operator (Mohammad). Thus, 'without Mohammad, there is no Islam.' That gets back to the point we made earlier. 'The doctrine requires humanity to imitate Mohammad in every facet of life.'[3] As I mentioned before, it is so demanding, many in the past actually chose to call it Mohammadism. This may be a lot more accurate from a Western perspective but is blasphemy in Islamic countries."

Sam said, "You see dualism more clearly if you apply a statistical analysis to the three documents in question. Their answer statistically is that the Koran has 153,000 words; the Hadith of Bukhari has 338,000 words; and the Sira has 408,000 words. So less than 20% percent of the doctrine is about Allah (the Koran) and the balance is about Mohammad (Sira and Hadith).[4] Such an analysis eliminates many questions and much confusion."

"That approach is certainly insightful," marveled Rick. "It paints a different picture of the Islamic faith in my mind."

Sam said, "Think of our conversation before Abe's arrival today, Rick. Now that you are aware of the term, can you recall anything in our conversation that could be considered as another aspect of dualism?"

Rick thought for a moment and said, "Well, you told me about the different revelations of Allah in Mecca and Medina. As I remember it, in Mecca, where Mohammad started his faith, they were peaceful and spiritual in nature because the movement was weak. In Medina, Mohammad came into his own and they turned to violence and warfare. Inasmuch as they came after the Meccan thoughts, they abrogated or cancelled Allah's previous declarations. But not totally!"

"Good, Rick, you are beginning to catch a glimpse of the significance. But there is much more," Sam added.

After a pause so Rick could make some notes, Abe went on, "Another critical area of duality comes with the division of people into the House of War (*Dar al Harb*) versus the House of Submission to Islam (*Dar al Islam*), in other words, the unbelievers versus the believers. In all the texts, Allah sanctifies violence for the complete domination of non-Muslims, who are required to submit. Non-Muslims are never considered to be the equal of the Muslim, although they may be respected. We'll get into greater detail about this when we discuss jihad.

"Of course, from the public's standpoint, probably the most visible effects of dualism observed in the West is the treatment of women in Islam, as highlighted by the wearing of special dress. There is much to be said about this issue, but it all boils down to their inequality with men before the law. Although it hasn't materialized in Europe, I believe women may well have a key role in resisting the rise of Islam in the United States."

After going over these points again and permitting Rick to ask more questions, Sam suggested that they grab Trudy and head for lunch. Rick said he'd heard there was an Olive Garden in Brandon and offered to foot the bill. They drove three cars because Rick had an appointment at the air base after lunch and Abe needed to check in at the store.

CHAPTER 8

Friday Lunch

Sam arrived first and asked the hostess for a table for four in a quiet section of the restaurant. When the others arrived, they were seated exactly as Sam had asked. The first thing Rick did was order a glass of beer. He said he felt as if he was getting the third degree and needed something to help him relax a little before his talks at the base. Both Sam and Abe chuckled while Trudy gave him a knowing look. She'd been through this before and knew there was much more to be discussed. Sam said, "We are only getting started; you might want to have two glasses." Rick shook his head, groaned, and smiled at the same time. After all, he'd asked for this.

During lunch, Abe casually asked what Rick was going to do at the base. Rick said that he was going to visit a couple of friends and try to determine if there might be a staff vacancy coming up in the summer he could fill. He told Abe he was a Reserve officer and it appeared he might be called to active duty around that time. He felt, as a result of his background and training, he might fit nicely into a Special Operations Command (SOCOM) staff position at the base, or possibly a J-2 (intelligence) position at Central Command (USCENTCOM). In either case, he knew his family would be happy if they came to Tampa. In fact, it would ease the pain of his recall.

He further explained that laying a little groundwork never hurt, particularly if someone in those headquarters believed he would be a perfect replacement in a specific job. Once he was definitely on the recall list, he could call the appropriate office in either headquarters and they could ask for him by name. It didn't always work smoothly or result in success, but it was worth pursuing since both commands would be ideal places for him to get some joint staff time. Everyone wished him well in his quest.

When Rick finished his comments, Trudy took the opportunity to remind everyone of the plans for the weekend. This afternoon, she knew Abe would finish his work with Rick. Tonight they would be together at their house for a Lebanese supper. Tomorrow George Ayoub would have additional discussions with Rick and Sam. Then the group would attend the Beirut Alumni Chapter supper at the home of Samir and Daud Shatila. Rick thought this was a great plan and said so. He was really pleased at their effort on his behalf and not hesitant in vocalizing it to everyone. He reasoned that coming to Tampa, the people he was being introduced to now would be welcomed into his family circle. As they finished lunch and went their separate ways, Sam asked that they try to be back at the house by three-thirty.

Before Rick got to his car, Sam pulled him aside and commented, "I know several people at both headquarters, and I'd be glad to put in a good word for you once you decide the type of an assignment you'd prefer."

"That would be great, Sam! I don't want you to say anything to Ann, but I'm really thinking SOCOM. I'd be one happy guy if I could get a job that had the possibility of a little action. I just don't want to sit at a desk for two or three years."

"With your background," Sam said, "I can't see you doing that either. On the other hand, you're not as young as you were the last time you were on active duty. Those old wounds give you any trouble?"

"No, I get a little stiff every once in a while but I have kept active running, doing my daily dozen, playing tennis and racketball. I believe I can keep up with these twenty-years-olds in any situation."

Sam chuckled and said, "Okay … not another word from me. You better be right, though. Wishes have a way of coming true, and you might find yourself romping through the bushes with twenty-year-olds before you know it."

"Nothing would please me more, Sam."

"I love to hear you talk like that, Rick. I agree with you whole-heartedly. This retirement is for the birds if you don't have something to look forward to in the morning. I learned that quickly. I haven't gotten around to telling you all the facts about my retirement. You know that I became an appraiser, but that's not all."

"Okay, Sam; I have suspected there was more to your fun in Florida than you let on, particularly with so much happening in the Arab world. I also ran into a friend of yours who confided that you seem to be doing a lot of traveling without Trudy. Actually, his comment was that you disappear occasionally, and his curiosity quotient goes up a notch each time. You know I have always understood your frustrations with the inability of our leaders to find a solution to the Middle East problem. At the same time, you have been so accomplished at emulating Arab Muslims, I always wondered whether or not Uncle Sam would truly put you out to pasture for good, or keep the strings pretty taunt." With a huge grin on his face, Rick went on to say, "There are situations where your talents—even in your declining years—would get you back into the action."

"All right, wise guy, you may question my receding hairline, but I'll give you a run for your money any day you want to check out my physical stamina and endurance. I'm still pretty agile and I'll bet I can keep up with you under any circumstances. Remember, a lot of the things we do rely more on brains than brawn. Didn't your dad ever tell you it's not the size of the dog in the fight, it's the size of the fight in the dog that counts?"

"Yeah he did," Rick said smiling, "but I also remember the day when all the brains in the world couldn't get the brawn very far down the road. In any case, you don't have to worry about me testing you at this point. I am more concerned about you testing me in some way I am not anticipating. You old codgers have a way of doing that when we are least expecting something."

"You may be right, Rick, but I'm easy. On the other hand, if you get one of the jobs I have been thinking about, you may get a chance sooner than you ever dreamed possible to test your mettle," chided Sam.

"Really!" said Rick as an inquisitive expression appeared on this face. "What do you have up your sleeve?"

"Sorry … I am not at liberty to say … I know that will raise the old curiosity temperature a bit higher, but I can tell you this. From time to time I have been called back for temporary duty when the higher-ups have thought that I might be useful in helping to resolve a specific situation. It's been great for me, and I've enjoyed every occasion. Can't say the same for Trudy, but she knows I'm in my element, and we have had great reunions in New York City. The longest I've been away at one time is six months, but that has only happened once. Most of the time it has been one to three months, and my involvement is very sporadic."

"What type of operations are we talking about?" asked Rick.

"I don't want to go into any detail. They have varied tremendously. There have been Military Assistance Study Groups, contract negotiations where my expertise has been helpful in resolving cultural issues, and helping with security coordination for visiting dignitaries. I have joined others in searching for and uncovering kidnapers or terrorists who have moved out of their safe havens, contacting old friends to help smooth the success of our activities in their countries, and helping to strengthen friendly Arab government agencies to counter the terrorist threat against both our country and their governments."

"It sounds to me as if you have been on the payroll more than you've been off," said Rick.

"I know," smiled Sam, "but I can assure you that I have been appraising property more than doing those things I just mentioned.

"Anyway, this is all by way of saying that you and I might have a chance to work together again once you are back on active duty. Would you be interested in tackling some assignments like these if you were given the chance?"

"You bet, Sam. It would be great to team up again, particularly if we had the promise of a little action to boot. But I am not certain how my background would be of benefit."

Sam didn't think about Rick's response very long. He said, "Come on, Rick, your Special Forces training would make you a natural selectee in several of these situations. But let's stop here. You've got to get to the base and I have to make a couple of stops before heading home. I was just checking the water to see if you were interested. You never know what lies around the corner. Don't worry, if I get a chance to suggest members of a team I am asked to be on, I'll be sure to mention your name if your presence fits in with our mission."

With a great sense of pride, relief, and excitement, Rick jumped into his car, fired it up, and drove off to the base. Indeed, he had made the right decision in coming to Tampa.

CHAPTER 9

Critical Features

Abe and Rick pulled up to Sam's at the same time. Both Sam and Trudy were anxious to know if Rick thought he might have been successful. His smiles told the story, but Abe wasn't smiling. He'd received a telex from this brother, Ahmed, which had changed his countenance. In fact, he stated it looked as if he was going to have to fly to Germany late Sunday or Monday.

Sam asked, "What's up?"

Abe responded, "I honestly don't know, Sam. Years ago, Ahmed and I set up a simple telex signal we could use to alert one another if trouble seemed to be brewing on the horizon for either of us in Lebanon. I'd completely forgotten about it until Ahmed telexed me that signal this morning. I don't know what the problem could be. Because of business and family, we have maintained contact over the years, but I really haven't been involved with his personal affairs. I visited him last month because of business. He seemed frustrated and a little tense for some reason. I thought it was the pressure of business. He did say he wanted to move to the United States soon and asked if he could stay with us until he got settled. Both Cynthia and I are happy and excited. We want him with us. I know this must be something serious because that signal means we need to talk in person. I have no choice but to fly out."

"Okay, Abe, just remember we are here if you need any help. I know this must be distracting. Do you feel up to continuing with Rick, or should we postpone our afternoon discussion?"

"No! I'd rather finish up because I do not know what my trip might lead to, and I really believe Rick needs to hear the rest of this." With this, everyone headed to the study with Trudy's coffee in hand. They got comfortable and down to business quickly.

"Well, Rick, as we discussed before our break, dualism is the key to understanding Islam. At the same time, there are two additional critical features in Islam that are foreign to Westerners. An analysis and discussion of them will help clear things up a bit more. The first deals with ethics, and particularly what it has to say about the interaction of Muslims and non-Muslims. If I asked you about ethics in the West, what would you consider to be the guiding ethical principle by which we govern our lives?"

"Abe, I'd have to say the Golden Rule, 'Do unto others as you would have them do unto you.'"

"Yes, replied Abe, we think in terms of a 'unitary ethic.' We want to be treated as 'human beings' that are equal before the law and in society. It was on this basis that democracy was created, slavery was ended, and men and women are treated as political equals."

"Of course we do, but there is a hitch," declared Abe. "All religions have some form of the Golden Rule *except Islam*.[1] As I've pointed out, Islam clearly establishes duality as a fundamental principle of its ethics.

"I am sure you understand that the principle of duality removes any possibility of applying the Golden Rule universally in Islam. What we have is one set of ethics for Muslims and one for non-Muslims. Of course, this probably happened after Mohammad moved to Medina. Unfortunately, this duality was also the basis for Mohammad's greatest single innovation: jihad."[2]

Rick couldn't resist and said, "I guess that depends on how you look at it. But with such ethics undergirding your philosophy, I can see how one could create, authorize, and support the prime duality of *Dar al Islam* (House of Submission) and *Dar al Harb* (House of War)."

"Yeah!" said Sam. "It's easy once you make such a differentiation because you have insured conflict between the two groups becomes an infinite and eternal goal. That's why Muslims can never give up their quest for domination. Allah told them to do otherwise.

"Rick, I know this is hard to swallow … but you have got to understand … the closest Islam comes to a universal statement of ethics is in the dictum 'the whole world must submit to Islam.'[3] This all-important statement leaves no doubt as to what Islam is about."

"I'm stunned," responded Rick. "I've never heard anything like this before. I don't believe anyone is teaching along these lines … at least not at my school. It seems to me without a concerted education program, we may be doomed to failure in dealing with Islam."

With some strength in his voice, Abe went on, "That isn't all! With dualistic ethics comes the second special feature: dualistic logic. This is particularly difficult for a Westerner to fathom because we believe in unitary logic. In other words, we believe all science is based on the 'Law of Contradictions,' i.e., if two things contradict each other, then one is false. That is not the case in Islam."[4]

"Holy cow!" blurted Rick. "I know you mentioned this before, but I think it is just now sinking in. Tell me if I am right: On the surface, this means that the Koran of Medina can abrogate the verses of the Koran of Mecca, but that both segments are still sacred, true, and usable because Allah is perfect and can't be wrong. Is that right?"

"Right!" replied Sam and Abe at the same time.

"That isn't all," said Abe. "Not all of the contradictions have been totally and completely resolved. You are right, however ... the bottom line is simply two things can contradict each other and be true at the same time. I suppose this is not terribly unlike situational ethics being taught in many places today. The one big difference, of course, is that we are dealing with Allah's doctrine. So, yes ... while two things may contradict themselves doctrinally, Muslims consider them both to be true at the same time. Their situation determines the doctrine which they will apply."

As Rick digested this for the second time, he muttered, "No wonder we have so much difficulty understanding Muslims. No matter what they say, if it is in the Trilogy, they can make a point that it's correct theology, and from their perspective, everything is fine. On the other hand, we stumble over their reality because we have not taken the time, or made the effort, to dissect the basis of their rationale."

Sam commented, "The support for the president's comment that Islam is a peaceful religion comes from such a rationale; however, the peace verse in the Koran is abrogated by the sword verse and any number of lesser but equally war-like and violent verses. This leads us to jihad and what the Trilogy is really saying about it."

Abe went on, "When the topic is jihad, moderate, nonconfrontational Muslims will play on the theme of jihad as an 'internal struggle.' Jihadists will also act like them when it is to their advantage. At the same time, this latter group will focus on the portion of the Trilogy that signals and supports all-out Holy War when dealing with other Muslims. We Americans gladly welcome the moderate position because it plays to our societal desires for harmony, unity, peacefulness, and stability. But is that position the true strength of the Trilogy?"

"I would guess by what is happening around the world today, it isn't," said Rick.

"You guessed correctly, Rick. But the key for all of us is what the texts say when they are properly analyzed. To ensure your understanding, let me emphasize that an analysis of the Hadith of Bukhari clearly shows that only 3 percent of those writings deal with jihad as an internal struggle, while 97 percent of the references concern jihad as Holy War. Additionally, 75 percent of the Sira of Mohammad is focused on jihad as warfare.[5] As a result, what the moderates say may be true, but the overwhelming evidence of the doctrinal texts provides greater credence to the jihadists.

"Rick," Abe continued, "I have no doubt that is one of the real reasons why moderate Meccan Muslims have not been able to counter the jihadists in any significant way during the four years of this war. The peaceful side of Islam is simply not its doctrinal strength. In fact, we must understand Jihad is not just Holy War ... it has always been complete and total war against civilizations and their cultures."[6]

Sam injected, "I know you have surmised by now this type of logic is completely foreign to the West, Rick. Unfortunately, our rejection of both Islamic ethics and logic creates an avoidance of learning about Islam because most scholars realize there is no compromise with dualistic ethics.[7] The absence of this type analysis within our intelligence community has been devastating to the prosecution of the War on Terror, in my opinion. You see, fundamentally, Islamic politics, ethics, and logic cannot be a part of civilization, as we know it. Furthermore, history and current events in Europe have shown that Islam does not assimilate, it dominates."[8]

Rick commented, "This doesn't leave us much hope, does it? It means there is no getting along with Islam because its demands never cease as it strives to bring non-Muslims into submission."

Sam nodded and said, "You know, there are many who believe that love conquers all. I am convinced it can, on a personal basis. Abe is a good example. On the other hand, I would venture to say that history and the Islamic role in it illustrates love does not conquer Islam."9

Abe went on, "That may sound like our worst problem but our naïveté has been equally absurd. Having failed to do our own analysis, one of our major problems has been, and continues to be, we have asked Muslims about their faith and they told us what they want us to hear. Not having studied ourselves, we have allowed their 'cultural experts' to do our thinking for us. Since Islam looks upon the West as its enemy, I know we have only been hearing that which deceives us into thinking Islam is harmless in all of its manifestations. Unfortunately, that is the initial stage of Islamic strategy under jihad when attacking nondiscerning countries."

"Yes," Rick acknowledged, "but my reading and observations have left little doubt we have failed to accept the statements of our enemies concerning their ambitions even though they have been made openly, promise sedition, and support violence and the overthrow of our government. Where is the sense in that?"

At this point, Abe said he could go on, but thought Rick had enough to absorb for one day and he needed to run home and pick up Cynthia for supper. "I would hate to be late for a good Lebanese meal," he said.

Everyone agreed it was time to get cleaned up. Rick headed to his room to call Ann and check on the kids. Sam went scurrying off to check on Trudy and the preparations for supper. He too had some things to accomplish before all the guests arrived, and he knew Rick would be down shortly to give Trudy and him a hand in the kitchen.

CHAPTER 10

Lebanese Supper

Promptly at seven, Sam and Trudy's guests began to arrive. Normally, people in the Middle East eat a little later, but Trudy knew Sam and the group had another big day coming and scheduled an earlier supper.

Rick helped get everything ready. He appreciated the opportunity to be alone with Sam and Trudy and talk about family and friends. The smell of the Lebanese food was tantalizing. He had learned to really enjoy the flavors. It had started with a couple of assignments to the Middle East, but Ann discovered a Lebanese restaurant in their hometown and they frequented it often. But this was going to be the piece de resistance. Trudy had mastered the fine art of Lebanese cooking. She had prepared sambousik, hummus, tabbouleh, shishkabob, dejaaj (chicken), baklava, and Arabic coffee. Rick was in seventh heaven just thinking about it.

In the midst of his musing, the doorbell rang. Rick and Sam got there at the same time. Abe and his wife Cynthia greeted them. Abe introduced his wife to Rick, and everyone headed for the family room; the doorbell rang again. This time, Sam said he would get it and left Rick with Abe and Cynthia. They hardly had time for two words when Sam returned with his other guests, George and Najwa Ayoub and their daughter Hannah. Rick expected an older-looking couple but both had Florida complexions and looked fit and about ten years younger than their true age. Hannah was a knockout by any standard. She was one of the most beautiful Lebanese women he thought he'd ever seen.

The conversation was in full swing when Sam entered the room with a tray of drinks. George was apologizing for not being able to spend the day with Rick and Sam, but said he was really looking forward to tomorrow. He added that he knew everyone was anxious to know more about the document Rick found in Atlanta, but he thought it could wait until morning. It was apparent he'd disappointed everyone. They silently agreed to abide by his decision; after all, it would only be a few hours.

Changing the subject quickly, George asked, "Rick, how is your education progressing?"

Rick groaned, "I'm being overwhelmed with knowledge and hope I can retain it all."

Abe butted in, saying, "I have a couple of wonderful books to recommend and I'll E-mail an annotated list to you when you get home."

"I sure appreciate the thought, Abe. I know I'll need more study … thanks."

With that, Abe told Rick he had a couple more points he wanted to pass along and would try to get them into the conversation this evening.

Changing the subject, Rick told the group there were no guarantees but it looked as if he might be able to land a job at either SOCOM or USCENTCOM. His previous military experience and current Reserve assignment appeared to give him some advantage. Because of his Special Forces work, he thought SOCOM might be the best fit. He was close to being promoted to colonel, and that was a possible problem, since there were not many positions for this grade officer at either command. In any case, he felt good about the visit with his friends, and he'd just have to wait and see what the Army did this summer.

Rick checked his watch and then excused himself to call Ann. Returning a few minutes later, he reported everything was fine at home and the news about his visits this afternoon really pleased her. Hannah asked if he had any children. He told her they had a boy, Rick Jr., who was twenty, and a girl, Cathy, seventeen. Hannah commented that she had just the reverse: a girl, Jacqueline, fourteen, and boy, John, twelve. She hoped that their families could get together if he and Ann came to Tampa. Rick asked if she was a good cook. She replied that she did a fairly good job. George said she was great. Rick said she didn't have to say anything else, she could count on any number of visits. Everyone laughed, and Trudy called them to dinner.

The meal was wonderful, and the common interests of all around the table sparked much conversation. Abe said he had called his brother because of the concern he had experienced when receiving Ahmed's telex. George asked what that was all about and how Ahmed was doing in Germany. Abe explained what happened and went on to say Ahmed was doing well, but he still wanted a face-to-face conversation with him as soon as Abe could arrange it. Because of this, Abe made reservations to fly out Sunday evening. He'd be in Frankfurt Monday morning and spend a couple days with Ahmed. He hoped to be back by Wednesday evening. Sam commented Abe would have a pretty darn short trip. Abe acknowledged the quick turnaround. Unfortunately, he had some important business to take care of in Tampa at the end of the week.

Abe's conversation reminded Rick that Ann told him of a call she received from Mark Fields. Mark was a bachelor Air Force friend from his Desert Storm days. He'd been a forward air controller who'd done an outstanding job while working with Rick's unit. For an Air Force guy, he was number one in Rick's book and had made a point to keep in contact.

Mark called to check in with Rick. He was assigned to the MacDill Base flying tankers on refuel missions around the world. He'd just gotten back to the States from the Middle East. Ann told Mark that Rick was in Tampa. Mark gave her his phone number and asked Ann to tell Rick to give him a call.

Rick knew he really wouldn't have time to see him with the schedule Sam had worked out. He asked the group if it would be appropriate if he invited Mark to join them at Samir and Daud Shatila's alumni supper tomorrow evening. Trudy said she'd check with them but knowing the way the Lebanese prepare for a social get-together, she doubted there would be a problem. Trudy said she'd call them after supper to make certain it was all right. Rick thanked her while reloading his plate with tabbouleh and hummus. Trudy and the women began clearing the table as Rick enjoyed his last few bites. It reminded him of home, and he marveled at how comfortable he felt in this group.

George asked Sam and Abe where they thought he should pick up with Rick's education in the morning. Sam said Abe had done a wonderful job providing the key points of political Islam in their discussion, and going over some of the important anti-Christian doctrine would probably be most helpful.

Abe agreed and went on to say although he'd explained the Trilogy of Islam to Rick, he hadn't emphasized the fact that the Bible is wrongly compared to the Koran. He assumed Rick got this message through the discussions, but since the Koran is only 14 percent of Islam's sacred texts, it does not contain nearly enough information to tell someone how to be a Muslim. In essence, the Muslim equivalent of the Bible consists of the Koran, the Sira (27 percent), and the Hadith (59 percent).

"I kind of got that message earlier, Abe," Rick said. "If the Koran only represents a small percentage of Islam's sacred texts, something is missing. I assumed that was the Hadith and the Sira. So, it takes the Trilogy of the texts to fully substantiate the doctrines of Islam."

"Yes, Rick," Abe said, "the Koran is similar to the Torah, consisting of the first five books of the Old Testament. The Sira compares to the Gospels, and the Hadith has similarities to the Letters. Measured by textural doctrine, Islam is 86 percent Mohammad and 14 percent Allah. But since Mohammad is the only person who ever heard from Allah, the Koran is really about Mohammad. Following this train of thought, one can say Islam is truly 100 percent Mohammad, although the mere mention of such a thought violates Muslim sensitivities and would be offensive.[1]

"Oh boy!" remarked Rick. "I understand ... but won't talk like that cause problems?"

George couldn't resist, "Based on the intimidation tactics used by different Muslim groups, it sure could; on the other hand, facts are facts ... and interpretations can always be different in a free society ... right?"

Everyone agreed. Abe heard the girls returning with dessert and quickly said, "And that is one of the reasons the Koran is specific in admonishing everyone not to challenge the words of Allah in any way. What Mohammad presented is very challengeable because of the way he lived his life, his willingness to incorporate pagan practices such as the Hajj rituals into his faith, and the co-opting of Jewish and Christian stories to meet his ambitions."[2]

Trudy had called Daud Shatila while Cynthia, Najwa, and Hannah busied themselves preparing the coffee and plating the baklava. As she entered the room, she told Rick he was welcome to bring Mark along tomorrow evening if he liked. "That's great," said Rick. "We've talked often but we haven't actually seen one another for the last couple of years. It will be good to touch base again.

The baklava was great but a sip of the Arabic coffee flooded Rick's mind with a thousand remarkable memories of his time in the Arab world. He really loved the people. Their hospitality and friendliness was the most gracious and wonderful he had ever received. His experiences had been exceptional until the ideas of Hassan el-Banna, Sayyid Qutb and the Muslim Brotherhood of Egypt, the Wahhabis of Saudi Arabia, the Salafasts throughout the region, and Al-Qaeda started to be lived out in the region and throughout the world by militants. The human tragedies fostered upon Muslims and non-Muslims were so unnecessary and wasteful.

As the women tidied up, the men headed to the screened porch with more coffee. Cigars were in the offering, although only George and Abe smoked. It didn't take long for the smoke to be noticeable even though there was a slight breeze clearing the air rather well. As they relaxed, George commented, "Speaking of Mohammad as the father of Islam and not Allah would not only trample on Muslim feet but also the political correctness crowd and the multiculturalists. In fact, I think they might be a greater threat to our nation than Islam. They are not familiar with the Trilogy, don't appear to make any concerted effort to uncover its truths, and simply accept what Muslims want them to hear. The propaganda they and the press allow to overshadow the truth in the name of tolerance and political correctness is absolutely astonishing. It is almost as if they are pushing for a Muslim takeover, as is happening in Europe."

"Yes, I've read about this," said Sam, "and I can't believe they don't understand the reality created under their noses. They just ignore it and play the appeasement card as different issues arise. They are behaving like the proverbial frog sitting in a pot of cold water as it begins to boil. Soon, it is overcome, having been boiled alive. I can't think of a better way to describe it."

Rick said, "Since 9/11, I have noticed a number of writers come up on the Net and question what is happening. Yet they can't seem to get their ideas into the mainstream media. We appear to be following in Europe's wake. Writers in Britain are being sued by a Saudi National for writing against Islam while many wrongs are being committed by militants to enhance the Islamic enclaves in the various nations. Intimidation is rampant and grows stronger. None of the immigrants desire to assimilate, and not much is being done to insure they do. Returning them to their home country doesn't seem to be an option the governments choose to employ. As their numbers increase, control is becoming more and more difficult, and the non-Muslim population is beginning to suffer from the Muslims' special treatment."

At this point, Abe said that Ahmed was disgusted with the events taking place in Europe and wanted to get to the States as soon as he could. However, Abe believed something else was causing his concern and was the reason for his telex today.

Just then the women entered the room and broke up the discussions, with Najwa announcing, "Everyone has a lot to do tomorrow, and we think we'd better be on our way home."

As George exchanged glances with Rick, he asked, "Sam, what time should we get together in the morning?"

Sam said, "9:30 to 10:00 seemed to work well today."

George nodded in agreement. Both Cynthia and Hannah said good night and headed for the door. Abe followed suit. Shaking his hand, Rick thanked him for all his help, and reciprocated as Abe gave him a typical Lebanese hug. With that, Rick turned and went into the house to call Mark about tomorrow evening.

CHAPTER 11
An Evening Walk

No sooner had the last car pulled out of the driveway than Trudy said she was going to turn in. After Rick finished his call, Sam said he wasn't quite ready to hit the sack and asked Rick if he would like to take a stroll around the block. Rick agreed and a minute later they were out the door.

Sam said he realized there just wouldn't be enough time to discuss everything he thought Rick should know about Islam. On the other hand, he hoped with a little additional reading, Rick would have sufficient doctrinal background for his articles as well as knowing when someone was trying to be deceptive. It was important he not have the wool pulled over his eyes through a lack of knowledge. Rick agreed with Sam and told him he would tackle a few of the books Abe was going to recommend.

Sam went on, "It is important to learn the Arabic words used to describe and discuss Islam. Westerners have a tendency to use their own words, and by doing so, every Arab knows they do not fully understand what they are talking about. For example, take the word 'kafir.'[1] Have you ever heard that word in the past?"

"No," said Rick. "What does it mean?"

"We've translated this word as 'unbeliever' in the West, referring to non-Muslims. While this is correct, it doesn't even come close to its true meaning to a Muslim."

"Do you mean our word is too emotionally and factually neutral?"

"Oh yes, Rick ... Kafir is so negatively charged in the Muslim mind, it is a wonder any Muslim will even address a kafir. There just isn't an equivalent word in English that is so dynamically bigoted. The worst part about all this for you and me is that Allah says we are kafirs ... it's not just a matter of a Muslim thinking this way or joking about us in this manner."

"That's scary, Sam. I mean, to think we are blind to the true meaning of any bigoted concept strikes me as being beyond reason, especially when you are dealing with people who are killing in the name of their religion at the same time."

"I agree. Although it's worse than you might think. The Koran tells us all about the kafir and leaves no doubt you and I are hated and despised by Allah."

"I guess if the shoe fits Allah, it should fit the faithful as well ... right?" asked Rick.

"Yes ... but the depth of the negativism is shocking, Rick. The Koran openly offers Allah's praise for all types of abuse of the kafir from torture, beheading, killing, terrorism, subjugation, and humiliation to outright war."

"That's definitely not neutral!" said Rick.

"No ... it's despicable ... just about every degrading term you can think of is used in the Koran when talking about the kafir. How does this sample make you feel: ignorant, blind, arrogant, evil, a liar, disgraced, a partner of Satan, doomed, detested, unclean, and cursed?"

"They get me hopping mad! So should we use the term kafir in talking between one another? It seems to me using it openly might serve to reinforce these terrible thoughts in the minds of our enemies ... couldn't this work against us in trying to resolve different issues?"

"Maybe so, Rick, but remember, the Islamist is already imbued with these thoughts ... they are a part of Islam he turns to every day when reading the Koran. No! We are the ones that need to understand which side of the fence we're on when it comes to these guys. That's the real problem ... the Islamists know their mind-set and we don't. This has to change before we lose a war without knowing the enemy we are really fighting. We need to know how they look at us and what Allah says."

'Won't information like this lessen the chances of our being conciliatory in exchanges with them? After all, if I get bent out of shape hearing it, won't others?"

"I don't doubt that for a second ... but at least you will be dealing with the cards you've been dealt and not a fake set that leaves you shaking your head in confusion and misunderstanding when things just don't appear logical," responded Sam. "From my perspective, that's good."

"Okay, so from your remarks I guess there just isn't a neutral description of the word 'kafir' in the Trilogy ... is that right?"

"Absolutely right! Each and every sentence using this word is negative, antagonistic, bigoted, and hateful. So when you come right down to it, 'kafir' is the real word we should be using. It shows our knowledge and unwillingness to be deceived. 'Unbeliever' is nothing but a Western-contrived, and thus misleading, word representing a denial of the doctrine. Remember what I mentioned earlier, kafir's uniqueness is enshrined in Islamic doctrine, and I can't emphasize enough Allah's words are considered to be sacred, absolute, complete, final, and the universal truth about all non-Muslims."

"Sam, I've read somewhere that the Koran says a Muslim is not to befriend a non-Muslim. This seems like a logical extension of the thoughts surrounding a kafir. In fact, as Allah defines a kafir, what Muslim would want to be his friend? Where does that leave us … if a Muslim is told he can't befriend and trust me, how am I supposed to befriend and trust him? I'm glad that not all Muslims follow the Islamists' approach to Islamic doctrine. Nevertheless, such doctrine is absolutely overwhelming to me. To think that Allah, a divine being, taught his people to look upon you and me and our families in that way is almost beyond my ability to comprehend. That is just evil!"

"Yes, Rick, it is almost inconceivable any god would teach his followers in this manner, but he did. Imagine being brought up believing those who do not think as you do fall into the kafir category. Even if you are not a militant jihadist, such thoughts color your outlook on the world around you. And it certainly explains the terrible actions of the fanatics in beheading kafirs before the TV cameras. We think it is barbarous, but in their hearts, they are following Allah's dictates."

"That is terribly depressing to say the least," said Rick. "It implies, from the jihadist's perspective, there can be no end to the conflict between us. It also implies the only way to live peacefully is to destroy the jihadists by conquering and controlling them, as was done after World War II. Those saying this conflict will go on for a long time aren't kidding, are they?"

"No, Rick, they aren't. And remember, Christians and Jews are not only kafirs but infidels as well. Christians are called infidels because they are not 'faithful' to the 'real' word of Allah, the Koran."

"I guess this means as a Christian I should never use any word except kafir because it will show I understand real Islam and reject the media's cotton candy approach to the whole subject."

"Yes, I'm with you, Rick, and I hope you will do this in your articles. I think it will mean more than you know and might help the timid become a little bolder in their approach to Islam over time."

As they walked on, Sam said he had one other concept and term he needed to explain quickly; he asked, "Have you read anything about dhimmis?"[2]

"It seems to me I have seen this word in one or two articles I've read about happenings in Europe, but frankly, I must have glossed over those sections because my memory is failing me right now," said Rick.

"Well, as you know, once Mohammad hit Medina, it wasn't long before he was fighting Arabs and Jews. Those captives becoming Muslims were no problem, but when the Jewish tribes refused to do so, he wound up with many captives and control problems. While many Jews were killed, he realized much talent and profit could accrue to Islam if he figured out a way to incorporate them into society."

"I remember now. After one of the first Jewish tribes was defeated, they executed an agreement with Mohammad called a dhimma."

"Good, Rick. This agreement established a second-class kafir citizenship status. As time went on, individuals living under such agreements were called dhimmis and the concept became known as dhimmitude. Of course, this unique political policy went right along with the concept of dual ethics we discussed earlier today. When you get into your books further, you'll discover this was a very effective technique for accomplishing Allah's directives."

Sam went on, saying, "Mohammad used jihad to crack open the culture forcefully, applied dhimmitude to replace it with Islam, and eventually destroyed the original culture by the oppressive policies applied to rule his captives. You have got to give him credit. He was highly successful."

Sam continued, "From what I've read, I don't believe any group of humans was as oppressed as the kafir dhimmis. Once placed in the dhimmi status, your choices were few: You either converted to Islam, fled to safety in another country, or died … there were many Muslims willing to help you choose one or three."

"To gain a better understanding, I'll have to read up on this, Sam. Recent TV, radio, and news reports have given me the impression that our European brothers appear to be falling into the dhimmi mind-set as Muslim immigration has exploded over the last thirty years."

"Yes, most of the European governments realized they had a declining population and opened their arms to labor from Muslim countries in the south. Unfortunately, they didn't plan well, and the immigrants have resisted assimilation in favor of their inherited culture. The Islamists among them encourage all to remain true to Islam and Shari'a."

"I guess that goes along with the multiculturalists who consider all cultures to be equal regardless of what they stand for or teach their people. That's asinine … I don't know of any culture that can match ours … only the Christian scriptures have absolute moral principles encouraging and supporting our free society," commented Rick.

"Trouble is, everybody wants to bring their cultural baggage along instead of living up to our motto, 'E pluribus unum,' out of many, one. And like the Europeans, we really aren't doing a very good job of changing their attitudes."

"I have gotten that impression from several things that have been reported recently," said Rick.

"Oops …, I'm sorry, Rick, we've drifted … time's short … and we need to get back to the dhimmi problem."

"Okay, maybe we can pick up on this again later."

With that, Sam said, "I'd encourage you to read more about the dhimmis in history. The degradation experienced by them as captives was complete, and it accomplished Mohammad's purposes very well. To the Muslims, paying a special tax and having one's civil and legal liberties curtailed was just payment for the protection their captives received from their captors. How do you like that logic?"

"I don't, but they seem to have been successful in selling it to the world ... that is, a world not strong enough or prepared to take action against them. I imagine the taxes filled Islamic coffers and made them rich while Islam was able to take historical credit for everything their captives invented or developed.[3] What about today, Sam? Is the concept being applied in the twenty-first century?"

"I believe it is, on a couple of levels. Today, dhimmis serve Islam by being apologists who only see the good in Islam and gloss over the facts and real dangers. I sense many have a secret fear of Muslims brought about by a lack of knowledge and jihadist tactics of intimidation. This is particularly true in Europe, but the Middle East Studies departments in our colleges and universities seem to be particularly prone to the apologist attitude. For the life of me, I do not understand why they distort historical facts and Koranic dictums to reach their conclusions."

"From what I've read, their agendas seem to be based on a calculated disinformation program engendered by the dictates of Allah to Islamize the world and the vast sums of Arab petro dollars their governments have available to propagandize and evangelize all of us. On the one hand, it's an outgrowth of the philosophy that the United States is the bad boy in the world, Christianity is obsolete, and anti-conservative progressive thought is dominant ... meaning diversity is streamlined as good. On the other hand, the economic need for oil seems to have put us in a subservient status that has the trappings of dhimmitude as the oil-rich states execute economic warfare against us in the quest for petro dollars and more control over our economy."

"I can't disagree, Rick ... but as a non-Muslim, I can take pride in being a kafir and infidel. I may be oppressed in captivity or even killed for my beliefs, but I am standing for my faith and culture. I cannot respect myself, nor do I deserve the respect of any Muslim, if I do otherwise. You have got to understand, being a dhimmi in the eyes of a Muslim is to be a coward in the undeclared civilization war in which we are engaged."[4]

"That's pretty strong, Sam. I don't think many would agree with you."

"Yes, I know ... just wait a few more years and closely watch what is happening in our country and the world. Our fellow citizens appear to be blind to the stealth Islamists of the Brotherhood, other Islamic organizations, and governments operating legally in this country. They are making calculated moves against our interests, and we are granting them the right to supplant our culture with theirs in many areas."

"Ah ... the symptom of the dhimmitude ..."

"That's right, and I am fearful for my children. Will my daughter be running around in an *abaya* or *hijab*, afraid to go out without permission and a male escort?"

"I see what you mean," said Rick.

"I just cannot see how you can overcome all this without a complete rewrite of the Koran. It is absurd to think Muslims would even consider doing so. It is Allah's word! On the other hand, a willingness to secularize and simply lay aside the political aspects of Islam seems to be the only solution on the horizon, aside from destroying those who are militants."

Rick thought for a minute and nodded, saying, "I don't think I'll be sleeping well tonight. Thanks, my friend, you have really made my day! That sure gives me something more to ponder. What outrageous and degrading concepts!"

As they approached the door, Sam chuckled, "You're welcome. Would you like something from the kitchen before you head to bed, or a shot of scotch? Both have worked for me in the past."

Rick said, "I'll have another piece of that baklava and milk. Maybe I can get a good night's rest after all."

"Oh! I almost forgot," responded Sam, "I plan on doing a run in the morning. Would you like to join me? After your comments last night, I thought you might be up to it."

"Okay, Sam, what time and how far?"

"Three miles ... what about a quarter to six?"

"You know how to hurt a guy ... but great! See you at 5:45."

With that, Rick headed for the kitchen and Sam went upstairs.

Trudy was already in bed. As Sam settled in, he said, "Trudy, an old friend of mine, Bill Tipton, called me just before supper. He asked that I spend a little time with him and a couple of his company representatives in Brandon tomorrow. Bill's company sells military hardware and training devices to foreign armies. He's asked me to join his company in the past, and I suspect he might do so again. If I am right, he'll want me to travel, and it might give us some opportunities to visit old friends in the Middle East and Europe."

"Sam, I know you well enough to sense your restlessness. The last six months have been very quiet for us, and your restlessness quotient has risen steadily, but I don't want you to get so involved that you become a workhorse again. At this stage of our lives, it just isn't worth it!"

"Okay, Trudy, I get your point. I'll hear them out ... you know I wouldn't do anything until we've talked. In any case, I'm curious as to why I'd be contacted at this point in my retirement. I can think of several possibilities, but let's just get a good night's sleep and see what the morning brings. Oh, by the way, don't say anything to Rick. If I like what I hear and we decide to do something, I can bring everyone on board when we have the details." Wrapping his arm around her, he whispered, "This is a perfect way to end a great day."

CHAPTER 12
Trudy and George

The next morning, following a couple of curt "Good mornings," they were out the door as planned. Settling into a jogging pace, the miles slipped by as both men settled down to business and hit their stride. Neither one evidenced any real strain or stress as they ended their run with a short sprint. Rick couldn't restrain himself and said, "Sam, you are surprising. Are you sure you haven't been running marathons or something? I swear you are in better shape than I dreamed. How do you keep so physically fit?"

Sam quipped, "The Army way … every day possible … you know, exercise, run, good diet, never let the weather interfere with your routine, and never say can't."

"Yeah! Yeah! Yeah! Just an old warrior who won't slow down. I swear you'll go to your grave shouting Jody's cadence at the same time," said Rick. They both laughed as they entered the house.

The exercise had been great, and as always, Trudy's breakfast left them feeling as if they wouldn't want another bite all day. As they were finishing, Sam said that he needed to look at his calendar because something was nagging him about his schedule. He checked it out and came back shaking his head. It seems he had told some of his buddies he'd help them for a couple of hours this morning, taking wounded veterans on a short field trip; he'd been so busy, he'd forgotten all about it.

He asked Rick if he would mind his absence for a couple of hours. He knew George would be along shortly, and he said he'd appoint a substitute, Trudy, who was better than he was when it came to Islam and Christianity. Trudy laughed and said she'd be glad to pinch-hit for the "master." Sam said, "It will cost me big time, but you'll be the benefactor, Rick."

George arrived a short time later and the three of them headed to the study. After everyone was comfortable, George said he wanted to delay talking about Rick's document until Sam was present. While they understood, it didn't make matters any easier, as their curiosity was at its peak.

George changed the subject, saying, "Being brought up as a Christian in Lebanon and other Middle Eastern countries was much different than being raised in the United States with the same faith. I believe Middle Eastern Christians are much stronger in their faith; they are more willing to suffer for Christ; and their ability to resist their Muslim persecutors is much stronger."

Rick said, "I can understand your conclusion, George, in light of the Iraqi Christian situation. They are being targeted every day but they remain staunch in their faith. I know many are fleeing to protect their families, but I suspect many will be back along with their Muslim contemporaries when things stabilize a bit."

George went on, "I don't believe Western Christians have the same resilience as those in the East. In any case, because of the constant persecution and their need to understand their Muslim neighbors, the doctrines of Christianity literally come alive in their daily living. If this didn't happen, conversion to Islam, with all the social 'advantages' it brings, would have been much more common. Today, as it was historically, Christian dhimmis have to have a deeply engrained faith to avoid the Muslim pressures to convert. Do you know what a dhimmi is?"

"Yes, George, Sam drilled me."

"Good … because there is no question Islamic pressures have been very effective in subduing the past enemies of Islam: the Hindus, the Buddhists, the Persians, and many Christians of the Middle East and Europe, especially when the repressions were more brutal."

"George makes a good case," commented Trudy. "Nevertheless, I suspect there are many more Christians in the West who would step up to the plate for Christ in the same situation. I believe this is true even though our society has run amuck in many ways. At least, I hope this would be the case. It is my belief that, in the face of Islam, each of us better know where we stand with Christ, or we will not be able to ward off the enemy as the world around us succumbs to the pressures we are most likely to receive."

With that, George said, "I doubt we will find many deluded Christians in the Middle East saying Christians and Muslims worship the same God, or we are both members of an Abrahamic faith. I hate to say it, but such statements are based on profound ignorance and drive home our Western penchant to believe that saying things often enough will cause them to be true. Herr Goebbels had a good propaganda idea during World War II but its one shortcoming was the truth when it came to light."

Rick said, "But in one sense, isn't that true? After all, both faiths are premised on worshipping one God and would seem to imply a certain degree of universality."

Trudy said, "Yes, they do, in the sense that both faiths have certain things in common. They both are based on the worship of one God. They also believe in his preeminence and in his supernatural powers."

Rick added, "I know as a Christian, I believe God is all knowing, all powerful, present everywhere simultaneously, and is above all dimensions in time and space. Since both faiths worship one God, I would assume this is also true for the Muslims."

"Right, Rick, but that is where the similarity of the doctrines ceases," replied Trudy.

George piped in, "Trudy is right. I'd agree if that was as far as we need to go; however, if the character, nature, and personality of God and Allah are not the same, then the Lord and Allah can not be the same.[1] Thus, it is impossible to be talking about the same God. I wish they were identical … that would be powerful, wouldn't it? Unfortunately, I can't emphasize enough … it simply isn't the case!"

Going on, George pointed out, "For one thing, Muslims do not believe Allah can exist in our material universe … nor do they believe an individual can have a personal relationship with him. In fact, this thought is offensive to them because everything they have been taught suggests such a relationship would make Allah subordinate to his own Creation."[2]

"That is the one thing about Christianity I love!" commented Rick. "I can have a personal relationship with my Lord. In fact, he seeks such a relationship with me and has left his Holy Spirit with us so that this might be accomplished in our lives."

Trudy said, "Allah lets his worshipers know what he wants of them but withholds knowledge about himself; therefore, in not being able to know Allah, Muslims must rely on an intellectual understanding as to who he is."

"I don't think there is much of a question about this," said George. "Nevertheless, the missing increment in the character and nature of Allah is the idea of love for humans in general. To be specific, there is no verse of compassion or love in the Koran mentioned or offered to a kafir ... dualism prevails and precludes it."[3]

"Now that I know something about dualism and how it is Mohammad who explains Allah's wishes," Rick said, "I can understand how devastating dualism really is when implemented. Without love and respect for all human life, we are barbarians," said Rick. "To be honest, I struggle with the Christian concept of 'loving my enemies' every day as I compare jihadist barbarism to our approach on the battlefield."

"Rick," George said, "I think we all do at some level, but we have our marching orders and I know you—like all of us—tend to follow them to the best of your ability ... after all, our final reports are going to be given to only one all-knowing commander, right?"

"Right."

"What disturbs me the most are former Christians in the United States, now Muslims, who talk about love as if it were engrained in the Koran just like the Bible," said Trudy. "Their ignorance is saddening. I am certain the Muslims who assisted in their conversion did not dissuade them from thinking this because it might cause them to think again. When you come right down to it, the average American has been brought up on Christian philosophy and wants to believe all religions are basically the same. I am reminded of the old adage, *'Buyer beware!'*"

"You mean there is nothing else in the Koran about love?" asked Rick.

"No," replied George, "there are verses talking about and demanding the love of fellow Muslims, the love of Allah, and Allah's love of his 'exemplary' followers, as well as family. Like Christianity, he also cautions about avoiding the love of money, power, other gods, and social standing … that's about it."[4]

George went on, "As a Christian, Rick, you are aware we are taught of God's love for all humanity and his love of the sinner but not the sin. Most importantly, while he exists apart from the material universe, he is also immanent. His presence and activity is within the world and human nature at all times. We can know him personally and those who know him intimately can walk in his presence."

"You know, George, there are some other things about Allah's character that trouble me just as much when dealing with kafirs," stated Trudy. "From what I have read in the Trilogy, he appears to be demanding, violent, greedy, spiteful, impersonal, judgmental, power seeking, capricious, arbitrary, heartless, and unforgiving, without the slightest grace or mercy.[5] The contrast with the God of the Christians is truly dynamic."

After a slight pause to let this sink in, Trudy said, "Before we take a break, George, many say Christians and Muslims belong to the Abrahamic faith. I know both faiths use the story of Abraham. There is an assumption made by many that we are talking about the same circumstances in both the Christian and Muslim rendition. What is the truth?"

"Basically, Muslims have co-opted the story of Abraham and Isaac from the Old Testament. Remember, Mohammad lived 570 to 632 years after Christ died."

"It seems to me that could make a lot of the things in the Koran suspect," offered Rick.

"In the Bible, it says that Abraham took his son Isaac, whose mother was Sarah, as a sacrifice for the Lord, and the Lord intervened by providing a ram in his place. Biblically, Isaac was Abraham's second son; however, he was the son God had promised Abraham … the one who would be the father of many nations." George added, "The oral Jewish traditions of this story go back some 2,300 years before Mohammad."

Rick piped up, "Do we have a chicken-and-egg story here? You know … which came first, or which is the true story?"

"Well, it does seem awfully convenient that Allah has the same story in the Koran but substitutes Ishmael for Isaac, with a different outcome. You'll remember Ishmael was Abraham's elder son, whose mother was an Egyptian slave, Hagar. As in the biblical story, Allah intervened and spared Ishmael, but according to Muslim traditions, he and Abraham went to Mecca and built the Kaaba. As a result of this rendition of their scriptures, Muslims say Christians, Jews, and Muslims are all part of the Abrahamic faith."[6]

Rick reacted, "I've heard this a number of times. Do you think this was one of Mohammad's ploys to help in converting the Jews?"

"Yes," said George. "He did everything to bring them into his fold and 'prove' Islam is true as being an extension of Judaism. He was clever. Genetically, there may indeed be a relationship between the two stories, but the key point recognized by the Jews was simply that spiritually there is no connection."

"Then how do you explain its acceptance by so many Christians today?" Rick continued.

"My personal view," George said, "is our scholars have let us down. It takes hard work to obtain the truth because of language barriers, and frankly, we like to be fed our information by 'cultural experts' rather than digging it out ourselves. The problem is your cultural expert may be a little short on his studies or may have a hidden agenda of his own, particularly when it comes to evangelizing.

"In any case, the media and many Christians have repeated this statement, thereby adding confusion to biblical history while giving credence to a deceptive Muslim utterance. You must remember, according to Islamic theology, the only way a Christian is actually an acceptable Christian to Islam is when he or she says (1) Mohammad is the final prophet of God, (2) Christ is a Muslim prophet, (3) the New Testament is corrupt, and (4) there is no Trinity. Significantly, only those Christians who admit this are members of the Abrahamic faith. All other Christians are not viewed as Christians, but infidels or kafirs."[7]

"Jeepers creepers," coughed Rick. "If I agreed to the Muslim version, I wouldn't be a Christian as I understand my faith. I'll bet there isn't one person in a hundred thousand of any faith who knows this! So those who talk as if the two versions are the same deceive us."

"At the same time, the acceptance of this deception and the broadcasting of it as politically correct and multiculturally sound assists the jihadists in undermining Christian theology and converting the unwary to Islam," offered George.

"Yes, and it's to your disadvantage because either way, you are a kafir with full dhimmi status."

"Let's take that break; I need to clear my head and exercise my legs. I think my brains have sunk to my seat. Is there any coffee left, Trudy?"

"Yes, come out to the kitchen."

George asked Rick about his friend, Mark. Rick said he had a lot of respect for Mark. As a young man, his family life was stressful. His parents had died in an accident and he'd lived with grandparents. When they passed on, he'd lived with an uncle. He and Mark met in Iraq before the first war started. Rick's A Team had been given a special mission behind the lines that started before the first forces crossed into Iraq. Mark had been assigned to the team in case they needed close air support. He'd been a real trooper and fit in perfectly. That had been very important since they jumped behind the enemy lines.

Rick went on to explain, "You always try to work with indigenous people friendly to your cause if possible, but sometimes you go in without contacting anyone. We had been dropped in to observe and report on enemy activity at a special junction of highways. It was a critical point because it was the fastest way to move armor and mechanized infantry forces to and from the battlefield for the Iraqis. It also was behind a significant defensive area of the Iraqis. My A Team was deployed on the high ground about 1,000 meters from those positions, but with our equipment we were in an excellent position to be very effective."

George commented that he was excited about some of the technological advances incorporated into today's new equipment.

Rick nodded in agreement and went on with his story, "As our forces advanced against the Iraqi defensive line, Mark went into action, calling air strikes on those positions. Concurrently, Iraqi reserve units began to head for that same defensive line. As they reached the junction, Mark turned his attention on them, and all hell broke out as our aircraft and artillery began to disrupt the various columns in and around the intersection. The Iraqis dispersed immediately. Most got off the road into the desert and headed for the front line, but one battalion-size unit headed toward our position. Mark calmly called in air strikes. It slowed them down somewhat but it also made them want to get under cover more quickly. We didn't want to expose ourselves too soon. So we held our fire as long as was prudent and then opened with everything we had available.

"They were surprised and immediately slowed, dispersed, and began to advance using fire and maneuvers. We knew we had the advantage defensively, but we also knew they had the numbers, firepower, and ammunition to overrun our position if they chose to keep coming. They did. Mark called in more strike aircraft and they withdrew.

"At this point, I had a decision to make. I thought we could hold off one, maybe two attacks but I needed to call for extraction. There was no way we were going to be able to outrun, or outgun, their armor and mechanized infantry, so I made the call and ordered some of the men to head for the LZ behind our positions with two wounded. Just about that time, the enemy started to advance again, and things got tricky. The fighters did a good job in knocking out several of the tanks, and our team took out two that got within fifty meters of our line. It was at this moment the incoming helicopter pilot called to let me know he was about ten minutes out.

"I ordered the rest of the team to head for the helicopter site. As I headed to the crest of the hill to take a last look, a mortar round landed nearby, and I got hit with shrapnel on my left side and hip. I was out of action. A couple of my men saw me go down and hauled me to the helo. They called Mark, told him what had happened, and turned the fight over to him and my senior NCO. Mark stayed in place until the last minute, and his efforts were wrecking havoc with the enemy. As the infantry dismounted and headed toward his position, he and my NCO left their concealment and dashed for the choppers that had taken us onboard. They made it just as enemy small arms fire began to hit the chopper. Their actions that day saved us all. Both of them received the Silver Star. I got a Purple Heart and a trip to Germany. I didn't see Mark for a couple of years. Ann was dying to meet the man who saved my bacon, and the first chance we got, she made sure I had him to supper. To hear her talk to her friends, you'd think she was running a dating business. She thinks he is a real prize—after me, of course.

Trudy said, "Okay, you two, it is time to get back to business. We have more to cover before lunch."

CHAPTER 13
Major Difference

"I'd better get back to our subject or Trudy will tell Sam I failed as a teacher. I couldn't live with that. Ha!" said George.

But without further delay, he launched into a discussion of the Trinity problem. "Rick, you know there is only one God in Christianity, and the Bible makes this very clear; however, he has three dimensions. In the Old Testament, we find God the Father, our heavenly Father, to whom Jesus prayed and who was so important to events of those times. Next comes Jesus the Son, who had an identical nature to that of the Father, lived upon this earth, and emulated his Father's desires. On the other hand, he is not considered a lineal descendant of God. Finally, Jesus left his Holy Spirit with us to indwell and empower all Christians while on earth. Without this concept of the Trinity, or three-in-one, you do not have Christianity."[1]

"I know," said Rick. "I have encountered many Christians and non-Christians who have stumbled over this concept, and I don't find it easy to explain myself, but I can accept it because it makes sense to me when I sit quietly and contemplate my faith and the way God has communicated with me, as well as the way he intends to communicate with me in the future. Truly, I have been overwhelmed by the significance of his grace when I consider he sent his Son to die for my sins."

George said, "Islam emphatically rejects the concept of the Trinity, and this is boldly stated in the Koran. Personally, I question whether or not Mohammad comprehended it himself. With his pagan background, illiteracy, and poor education, I believe he was more inclined to think in terms of multiple, separate, and distinct gods when the Christian Trinity was mentioned. Be that as it may, a concept of the Trinity does appear in the Koran although altered to fit Allah's concept. It seems the key figures in the Islamic triangle are Allah, Mary the mother, and Jesus the son. Mary conceived Jesus when Allah simply called him into being in her womb. The Koran also refers to Jesus as a man with limited prophetic powers granted by Allah while on earth. It goes on to say he was not divine and he was not crucified. Judas was crucified instead."[2]

"Gosh! George, that is one heck of a big difference! You have to accept the idea that since Mohammad came after Jesus, he was either the final prophet or a false one. I am beginning to see why he hated the Christians and Jews of the time. I understand they told him nothing in his life demonstrated he was a prophet, let alone the final prophet, and he responded by attacking them every way he could. Think of the millions of people who have died just because of this."[3]

Trudy added, "The net result is the other part of the story. Allah through Mohammad launched into a tale calling the Bible a 'corrupted document' because it did not contain the messages of Allah as set forth in the Koran and it did not say anything about their belief that Mohammad is Allah's final messenger."

George couldn't help himself and said, "Trudy's point is important because the talk of a corrupted Bible won't go away. You see, Allah and Mohammad arrived at the concept of a 'corrupted Bible' by stating Islam … and only Islam … had been the religion of all peoples since the beginning of time. Thus, all the other religions had sprung up after Islam and because they did not follow the dictates of Islam, they amount to nothing more than a corruption of Islam. Using this logic, Mohammad and Allah went on to say the corrupted religions needed to be eliminated in any way possible. Thus, to Allah and Muslims, the aggressors against Muslims are those considered to be corrupting the faith by following other religions. Reasoning like this allows all Muslims to consider themselves on the 'defensive' when encountering any direct, indirect, real, or perceived actions against Islam."[4]

"I understand the logic," said Rick. "What a bold and gutsy approach! In a single stroke, you co-opt all the religions of the world and place Islam at the pinnacle."

"That's right," agreed Trudy. "However, there is no historical evidence to support such a viewpoint, only the word of Allah through Mohammad. For the Muslim, it's all powerful, but for the thinking man who looks for evidence of support, none is apparent."

"I guess any story can be successful when there is absolutely no way to refute it except common sense. At the same time, anyone who tries is attacking Islam and Allah's dictum not to do so. Right?" asked Rick.

"That's right, but there are a couple of other things about Mohammad worth considering. Mohammad told everyone he was a normal man, a Warner, i.e., in the sense of warning others they were on the wrong track, preaching one god and evangelizing all non-Muslims. He also said he was a sinner. He acknowledged he performed no miracles, although others since have claimed otherwise in defending him. To me, the fact others later claimed he had performed miracles demonstrated their need to compare Islam favorably with Christianity. Lastly, Mohammad said he wasn't certain Allah would permit him to go to heaven. It does seem unusual that a messenger from Allah would question whether or not he was going to Paradise for eternity."

"That would sure make me feel uneasy," said Rick. "I mean, if the messenger of Allah isn't sure he will go to heaven, where does that leave the average Muslim?"

"Personally, I believe it leaves those who really think about their religion with some big doubts; however, let's leave this right now. We need to move on. Without going into details, let me just observe that all the biblical stories have been changed to fit Allah's purposes in the Koran. The story of Abraham is classic, but I am going to allow you to discover the others on your own time using Abe's bibliography. I'd rather spend our day on a couple of other important concepts."

"That's fine, George."

"Before we close the thoughts of corruption out of our discussion, I'd just like to say, I believe Mohammad took what he wanted from the existing religions. He put the selected items into his view of what a religion should and could be to achieve the power and results he wanted. In this, he was masterful because his new religion incorporated many aspects of pagan worship that the Arabian tribes already knew. For example, Allah was the chief deity in moon god worship, the rituals used at the Kaaba were those he incorporated into the Hajj,[5] the self-image of the Arab as a warrior was cardinal to Islam's militancy, plunder was an economic incentive of huge proportions, and all of these aspects of the faith helped contribute to a new political sense of Arab unity. Worst of all, Allah actually sanctioned every form of violence to overcome the other religions of the world."

Rick mused, "It is hard for me to believe a religion would incorporate a rationale for violence, separatism, forced conversions, and inequality into its doctrines, and yet that is exactly what needs to be made clear to the American people. It is also one of the most striking points of contrast with Christianity. Jesus came that we might have life and live in harmony with others. He died for us, but Allah asks his followers to kill and be killed in his name. I cannot think of a more dynamic contrast."

Just then, the telephone rang. Trudy dashed off to answer it while George went over a couple of points with Rick. When she returned, she said the call was from Sam. He wanted them to know he would be free for lunch and he'd buy if they would meet him at Chili's in Brandon. Everyone agreed they would go anywhere if Sam would buy. Trudy called him back and told him they were on the way.

In the car, George said that Rick and his friend Mark certainly had an exciting few moments in Iraq. He asked how the other members of the team, particularly the two wounded Rick had mentioned, were doing. Rick said both had recovered and were back in the line. George asked if he missed the action involved with a small unit, and Rick admitted that he did. He commented there was something about being with a group of good guys who all had their act together and were facing a common challenge that made you feel special. The bonding was truly significant. That was one of the reasons, he admitted, he still maintained contact with them.

Trudy acknowledged the importance of such relationships. She knew Sam really enjoyed his reunions. From her perspective, the banter that ensued was ridiculous, but she loved to meet the people and had enjoyed accompanying him.

Rick asked George about his family. He said he and his wife were so happy to be in the United States with their children. They both missed Lebanon and the way of life they had there prior to the civil war. It had been a predominantly Christian country politically and demographically, but for a number of years, it also teetered on a Muslim population majority. Everyone had gotten along pretty well, although talk of coming changes did enliven many conversations. In any case, both he and Najwa longed to visit their families although Lebanon didn't seem the place to be these days. Rick acknowledged it was probably best to stay away in the hope things would get better in a few years. George said he was getting tired of waiting.

Trudy asked about his son. She and Rick had met Hannah but not Thomas, who was several years younger. George offered that Thomas had gotten out of law school two years before 9/11 and joined the FBI. His background and knowledge made him an asset to his office, as the War on Terror got under way. He'd been working out of the Atlanta office recently; however, George knew he was trying to get to Florida, but it didn't appear such a transfer might happen soon. He'd married a redheaded Virginia girl by the name of Alice, and they had two young boys. George suggested it would be great if Rick could meet him on one of his research trips. Rick asked for his information and told him he'd definitely look him up.

As Rick finished speaking, George pulled into the restaurant parking area. They saw Sam standing at the front entrance and dropped Trudy off so she and Sam could get a table. The place looked a little crowded.

After everyone was seated and had a chance to review the menu, Rick said he was going to have a chicken taco because he wanted to save room for the anticipated meal he would receive at Samir and Daud Shatila's this evening. Everyone agreed with his moderation and did the same.

Sam asked how things had gone during the morning. Rick commented that George and Trudy had done a great job. In fact, if Sam wanted to take a nap this afternoon, he thought George and Trudy could handle the remainder of his research without any problem. Sam said he recognized some favoritism in Rick's subtle remark, but he thought he could get through the afternoon without a nap, and from his perspective, it would be great if Trudy continued to participate. Trudy said she'd see how she felt after lunch. She was certain the three of them could handle the afternoon session without her.

George asked Sam how his morning had been. Sam said that being with the severely wounded was always inspirational for him. Most of them wanted to get back to their units but may never do so because of the damage to their bodies. On the other hand, their spirits were such that most would carry on with life undaunted by their physical handicaps. In any case, it had been a wonderful morning, and he looked forward to following a couple of them closely while they were at the VA hospital.

The food arrived as Trudy asked Rick about Ann. Rick said she had taken a job at the local high school as a substitute teacher. This gave her an opportunity to interact with their two daughters during the day and be home with them in the afternoon. Rick, Jr. was at Georgia Tech studying engineering and participating in ROTC. All the kids were doing well, and both he and Ann were well pleased.

"That is good to hear," said Sam.

"Yes," said George, "I am sure you are proud of them. There are a lot of temptations out there. It's always wonderful to hear good reports." Everyone agreed. The waitress brought the bill and everyone pointed to Sam.

CHAPTER 14

Sam's Surprise

On the way home, Sam told Trudy he'd spent a couple of hours with Bill and some of his staff before catching up with the veterans.

Trudy couldn't wait for a further explanation and blurted, "What did they want, Sam?"

Coyly, Sam smiled and said, "Me … it's kind of an interesting story."

"I'll bet it is," said Trudy. "It seems to me your stories have been getting longer and longer these days."

"Trudy, that isn't fair. Give me a chance to explain …"

"All right," she sighed with a smile.

"When I got to the restaurant, Bill had two other company officials with him. After introductions and ordering a cup of coffee, he said, 'Sam, you and I go back a long way.'

"I laughed and told him, 'We sure do, and if our hairlines are any indicator, I'd say too far back.'

"'That may be so,' he said, 'but I remember your work well. Old dogs may not be able to keep up with the young ones physically, but you can't beat their experience, and by the way, you appear to be in great shape.

From our days in Afghanistan not so long ago, you know as well as I do that the tribal elders, or "White Beards," have the respect the younger men never can muster.'

"'Yes, I do,'" I said, "'but you didn't come here to talk about White Beards and Afghanistan.'

"'Well,' he said, 'in a way I did. Let me explain … I am very familiar with your work throughout the Middle East. Our paths have crossed too many times for me and my staff to be oblivious to the work our government has asked you to be a part of in the past. You're a natural because of your education, language, understanding of the culture, and numerous friends you have cultivated in the various Arab countries. So, yes, I consider you a true White Beard amongst your Arab friends and acquaintances.'

"'I am flattered, Bill,' I said, 'but …'

"'You know that our company is involved in the sale of small arms, ammunition, and training devices to the military around the world. I know that you do not want to be involved in such activities because you have turned me down before; however, some things have happened recently that I hope will cause you to change your mind. And, by the way, before I get into the details, I want you to know that I have checked with our civilian and military friends in Washington before calling you.'

"'Obviously, you got a green light …'

"'Yes, I did,' he said, 'along with enthusiastic support for your participation.'

"'Boy, you sure know how to lay it on … Go on …'

"'First,' he said, 'you possess outstanding contacts throughout the Arab world that could help smooth the way for our business. People you know from your AUB days, your assignment days in Jordan, and your many missions into the area are now in positions of significant, if not great, responsibility within the civilian and military offices of the different governments. As a result, you could be of great value in helping us get behind some of the closed doors we have experienced over the years. You do not have to sell a thing ... just help us meet the right people and get to the decision makers. No one knows the techniques of selling to these countries better than you. Small arms are small arms, but frankly, our training devices are second to none. Competition is keen and every bit of help is worth its weight in gold. We would pay you $100,000 per year with a bonus that depends on the contracts you help us nail.'

"'Gees, Bill!' I said. 'That is one enticing offer, but you know I am against using my contacts to advance arms sales regardless of the money involved. I am not against the sale of defensive weapons. There are plenty of guys doing it. I am more concerned about my contacts and placing them in positions of conflict within their own departments.'

"'I understand,' Bill said, 'but what about training devices? We really have developed some of the best in the world. They speak for themselves once we can get them demonstrated, but we have to get in the door. Helping us with this type of sale shouldn't give you the same problem.'

"'The competition is just as tough,' I said. 'You're right, though, I don't think my friends could have as many problems.'

"'Sam,' he said, 'we'd love to have you join us. You and Trudy could take some trips back to your old stomping grounds. I am certain Trudy would like that and you'd have some extra cash to make it all work.'

"I said, 'I'll talk to Trudy, Bill.'

"He said, 'Great! We want you to be comfortable in anything you do for the company. That's why I broached our business needs first. Now, I want Jim and Frank to spend a few minutes introducing you to the real reason we are having this conversation. Of course, what I am telling you now is highly classified and you know the rules.'

"'Bill,' I said, 'you are a louse. You buttered me up and got me thinking how great it would be to do some traveling with Trudy and now you're about to throw a monkey wrench right into the middle of my wonderful thoughts and upset my whole dream. Couldn't we have saved this until I talked to Trudy?'

"'No, Sam, I wanted you to have the complete story before you said yes. We've been friends too long for me to pull the wool over your eyes.'

"I said, 'I appreciate your enticements and your honesty, I was just hoping for once there would not be a string attached. Okay, let me have it.'

"With that, Bill nodded to Jim and Frank to begin their briefing. It seems that good intelligence information had been received from our agencies in Iraq, Afghanistan, as well as the embassy in Pakistan. As the pieces of the puzzle were gradually assembled, evidence mounted as to a number of key Al-Qaeda operatives and combat leaders in their organization. Some of these men are well educated and graduates of Beirut universities. Although their dates of attendance varied, the thought was that some had attended during our years in Beirut or have children who are involved with the terrorists. With that, Jim had produced about ten pictures and asked whether or not I recognized any of them. I identified four of them.

"Bill then asked, 'Sam, I know that you have visited with some of your classmates over the years. Do any of these men fall into that group?'

"I responded, 'Yes, all of them.'

"Bill offered, 'Not all of them are believed to be Al-Qaeda representatives. They may all be members of the Muslim Brotherhood, but that is unconfirmed. On the other hand, one is thought to be a higher-up in Hezbollah, another in Hamas, and two with Osama. Interestingly, all four recently left their safe havens and have been traveling extensively throughout the region and into Europe. One even made it to the United States. Our theory is they are participating in various coordination and planning meetings with the leaders of jihadist groups concerning forthcoming strategic and tactical operations against Arab and Western targets, particularly those countries helping us.'

"I injected, 'Based on my past experiences, I'd say that was a pretty good assumption.'

"Bill commented, 'The extent of movement is a relatively recent phenomena and is what caught our attention. Of course, our concern is focused on why it is happening. It could be innocent enough, although all of my guys and those in Washington believe extensive coordination and planning of this type implies something bigger is brewing than we have seen previously.'

"I commented, 'Okay, you have made the identifications, developed the background information for these characters, and know that they have been my friends over the years. So what now?'

"Bill replied, 'I am not certain we really know. A lot of the information we need in terms of their actual involvement with these different organizations has not been uncovered as yet. Some of their travels could be innocent enough, or they could be having a dangerous rendezvous. In the latter case, they may need to be captured, or at least operationally stopped. One or two need to be watched closely. It is possible they could lead us to additional operatives or information that would be extremely important to countering their plans.'

"'So, Bill,' I asked, "what does this have to do with me?"

"'Well,' he said, 'everyone believes that as an employee of the company, you would have good reason to move freely throughout the area. With reliable intelligence, we could probably insure that your path would cross with those of your friends during their travels. At the same time, you would be free to contact them to renew the old friendships you had previously and interact as you saw fit. Who knows what information could be uncovered in the process? As the situation firms up a bit, there would undoubtedly be specific bits of knowledge we would seek to acquire. Hopefully by then, the relationships would be such that any marginally sensitive questions would not cause a concern.'

"I said, 'Sounds like you guys are placing a big elephant on my back. It would take me some time to come up to speed on your training devices, and it sounds as if we'll need a number of people on our team to keep abreast of all this movement.'

"'You're right, Sam,' he said. 'We'll be setting up a small task force focused on this mission."

"'Can I choose some people I've served with previously to work with me on this,' I asked, 'particularly the teams that would be involved in the capture or destruction of a target?"

"'Sam, we look forward to your input,' Bill said, 'but you know we cannot guarantee anything.'

"'I understand,' I said. 'How long do you expect this operation to run?'

"'Once we get this set up,' he said, 'I tend to believe it will be permanent. You may be the White Beard and fall out at some point in time, but you'll be training and introducing others to the game along the way. Hopefully their beards will grow long enough before you depart so that a seamless transition can take place. By the way, I wouldn't want you traveling alone. Things can get a little dicey very quickly, and I think partnering is the best way to go these days. Of course, there may be times when this is not possible, but I would hope they would be the exception and not the rule.'

"I chuckled and said, 'Trudy will like that, but then asked whether it was because of my age or my great value?'

"Bill retorted with a laugh, 'Now that I think about it, I'd say age … value never entered my mind.'

"I said, 'Guess the truth had to come out sometime. You know how to hurt a guy … and a friend at that.'

"'Yeah!' he said. 'Sam, sometimes the truth hurts, but it is always better to get it out in the open!'

"'That's okay,' I said. 'Trudy will agree with you and you don't want her on an age kick if you want me on the team. I am not sure I could handle her nagging. Right now I am just hoping that you've sweetened the pot enough that I will be able to pacify her. The money won't be as big a selling point as accompanying me on trips. I'll play it for all its worth, just don't mention age. Okay?'

"'Okay!' he said. 'I didn't know you were a wife-dominated old man though. It's amazing what we learn through these interviews.' And everyone laughed.

"With that, Bill said, 'Sam, it's up to you. We really need your help. We all understand you are retired. Nevertheless, the contacts you have are the ones we need to verify as being friends or working for the enemy. This is my cell phone number. I'd like an answer in a week, because one way or another, we need to get the ball rolling.'

"'I think that's doable, Bill,' I said. "Let me go over all this with Trudy. We'll both need to mull over the full extent of your offer and what it will mean for both of us as well as our family. Frankly, I'm game but the years are flying by at a pretty rapid rate. I missed a lot of time with my kids chasing all over when they were growing up, and I promised myself I'd try to make up some of that time in retirement.'

"'Boy,' he said, 'if there is one thing I understand, it is your last point. Look on the positive side. There is nothing that says you can't take your kids on some of your trips, as well as their kids. What an education they would acquire! Not many granddads can do that for their whole family. But you could; just think cruising down the Nile, horseback riding in Petra, swimming at Club Med on the Red Sea coast.'

"'Man!' I said. 'You sure missed your calling, Bill! You should have spent your time in marketing. Enough! I'll get back to you in a week, if not sooner.'

"'Sam,' he said, 'it's been good talking to you again.' We shook hands around the table and over his shoulder Bill said, 'Give my best to Trudy,' as he walked out of the restaurant."

As they drove along, Sam tried not to miss any of his conversation with Bill in relaying it to Trudy. He used everything he could to entice her: the travel, the money, his freedom of movement and scheduling, and the inclusion of the kids' families in the travel. She listened intently and finally said, "Sam, I have been with you too long. It all sounds too good to me. There is something else going on here, but I do not need to know more than you have told me. You have played 'spook' too often in the past and I have no doubt that given the chance, you would do it again in a heartbeat. So knowing that you sell training devices is enough for me except for one thing: You better be good at it. I'd hate to have you lose that salary."

They both laughed and Sam countered, "I understand the shopping is great in Abu Dhabi, Dubai, and Oman. Seriously, though, I am already looking forward to visiting with some of my old friends. Some of them occupy high positions in their governments. To be honest, I don't know how some of the ones I went to school with ever got to where they are in their careers, but it will be fun to visit and figure it all out. I know you enjoy the ladies, and I am confident reestablishing friendships is something you'll really enjoy."

"Okay, Sam, you have always known how to get to me and with promises like that, my hard line softens quickly. But don't you forget Jordan and Cairo are two places we must visit often."

"It's a deal, honey. We'll make it happen."

"You'd better, Sam Flynn, or your name is mud."

With the decision made, the two of them arrived home, agreeing that they would not tell their guest or their Lebanese friends until things were more definite. Sam also told Trudy they should both take a couple of days to think and pray about it before he called Bill. They'd talk again before he made that call. They both wanted to be absolutely sure they were making the right decision.

CHAPTER 15
Saturday Afternoon

Rick and George thanked Sam again for lunch as they settled in their chairs. Trudy had begged off this session, saying she had a lot of things to do before the Shatilas' party that evening.

Now that the three of them were together again, George said he'd like to spend a minute telling them about Rick's document. But first he asked if either of them had read much about the Muslim Brotherhood.

Sam said, "Some time ago, I read the Brotherhood had become a very effective covert organization since its beginning in 1928, under the motto: 'Allah is our objective. The Prophet is our leader. The Koran is our law. Jihad is our way. Dying in the way of Allah is our highest hope.'"

"A motto like that gives me a lot of heartburn," said Rick. "In its own way, it sanctifies the jihadist approach to evangelizing in Islam and reinforces death if needed as achieving their goal."

"Couldn't agree with you more, Rick," nodded George, "but that's not all. The Swiss authorities raided a luxurious villa in Campione, Switzerland, on November 7, 2001, at the request of the U.S. government

103

and found a document published in 1982 during the Brotherhood's re-chartering process, called 'The Project.' It represents a flexible, multiphased, long-term approach to the cultural invasion of the West and calls for the use of everything from immigration to terrorism. The aim of the writers is to progressively infiltrate, confront, and eventually establish Islamic domination over the West."

Sam said, "I'm aware of that, George … and it's scary as heck … to think such a well-thought-out master plan has been in existence for twenty years before being uncovered … talk about security and intelligence failures. In truth, I believe everyone was flabbergasted by this latter fact as well as its effectiveness in Europe. Obviously, it was highly classified at first, and like all such discoveries, it has taken some time for the information to filter into the media. Unfortunately, they have not done much with it."

"Anyway, Rick," George said, "the document you found was written nine years later and basically represents the Brotherhood's cultural attack plan against the United States. We have had a copy of the U.S. version for some time, and the one in the airport was identical to it. While it is not new in the intelligence community, our technical boys are going over the envelope and document with a fine-tooth comb to see what we can learn about the person who left it behind. Whoever it was, I imagine he or she is very embarrassed and in hot water at the same time. The most obvious clue we have right now is the partial handwritten return address on the envelope. It has been pretty well mutilated but the last three numbers of the ZIP code are legible, along with a couple letters in the street address. Importantly, that gives us a clue the document may have started in the Tampa area, or at least someone in the Tampa area has had contact with it. We've had indications of some activity in the Bay area before but nothing we have been able to sink our teeth into.

In any case, we are on top of this. I will try to keep you informed as developments occur."

Sam said, "Well, Rick, it appears your Boy Scout effort has paid off in ways you never anticipated. Aren't you glad you were curious?"

"I sure am, Sam. Maybe I'll get an exclusive on this story."

"The FBI' s pretty careful about releasing information. You'll have to twist some arms for that."

"It sure will give me a chance to see how much influence my editor, Ed, has in Washington."

With that banter behind them, Sam and Rick thanked George for his rundown on the document, said they hoped some good information would come from all this, and returned to George's teaching with a short review of the morning's activities for Sam.

George opened by telling Sam that he'd ended the morning session with the Islamic theory of biblical corruptness. Sam knew his thoughts. From George's perspective, the concept of corruptness should really be applied to the Koran and the other Islamic supporting documents. With Sam on the same sheet of music, George went on to say he needed to talk about the totality of power attributed to Allah in all Islamic doctrinal writings.

"As you know, Sam, Rick will discover the reader finds the omnipotence of God emphasized over and over in the Koran to the extent that man's will is totally subordinate to Allah's."

"Do you mean doctrinally an individual really does not have a will of his own?" said Rick.

"That's right," said George. "In fact, even those who disbelieve do so because Allah wills it."

"In today's world, I find it hard to believe people actually follow such doctrine," said Sam. "We are talking about an overwhelming and uncompromising fatalism."

Rick injected, "I've known fatalism was part of Islam because I have heard countless Muslims say, '*In shah Allah*,' if God be willing, in response to everything from a business transaction to a proposed supper appointment. More often than not, it seems to be more of a rote response based on habit than meaning, but I guess one can never be sure."

"No," replied George. "And just think how powerful that was in the minds of the Arab warriors of the time. One Koranic verse even says, 'God killed them, and those shafts were God's, not yours.' The meaning is clear: 'You will not die unless Allah wills it,' and in other portions of the Koran, if you die in battle you will go straight to paradise."

"Oh! That could be a good incentive, if it means you go straight to paradise. I assume that paradise is the Muslim expression for heaven," said Rick.

"Yep,' said Sam, "and that's what Allah and Mohammad taught their followers. It is a powerful teaching even today, look at the suicide bombers and the intellectuals who succumb to this doctrine; in fact, being killed in battle is the only way to absolutely guarantee you're going to paradise. And should it happen, many of your family and relatives rate the same treatment."

"I suppose the bottom line is everyone strives for paradise," Rick said, "but my impression is doctrinally the focus is truly on the warrior."

"You're right, Rick," George said. "This is just another tremendous incentive for the Believer, and it undergirds the militant nature of Allah's doctrine."

"Obviously, free will is not as key an ingredient in Islam as it is in Christianity," said Sam. "I know you understand the Christian viewpoint, Rick, so I'll stop here, but I wanted you to have a good understanding of Islam in this regard."

George said, "I think Rick has the idea, Sam; I'd like to move on in the interest of time. I think we probably should discuss the concept of sin in both faiths, because the story of Adam and Eve is in both the Bible and Koran. The concept in the Bible is that God created us sinless; however, Adam and Eve disobeyed God, believed Satan in the garden, and sin entered the human race from that time forward. Thus, we all carry the burden of a sinful nature that was overcome by Christ when he was crucified on our behalf. At the same time, God gave us 'free will' and the ability to obey or disobey his teachings. Obviously, following Christ in our daily lives is the answer to overcoming our sin nature. Not only that, but Christ intercedes for us all the time. Nonetheless, Christians are saved by grace and not by any works."

Sam nodded in affirmation and said, "Essentially the same story about Adam and Eve is in the Koran, with one major exception. Sin as understood by Christians did not play a role in their fall. According to Islam, human beings are not born with a sinful nature. They come into this world with an excellent nature."

"Yes," declared George. "Muslims understand that they may exhibit moral weaknesses as they go about their daily living, as did Adam and Eve. Thus, regardless of being kicked out of the garden for eating fruit, Adam and Eve never found themselves separated from Allah. They are considered Muslims by birth only to become tarnished by their worldly environment."[1]

"So how do they overcome their moral weaknesses in order to get to paradise, beside dying in battle?" said Rick.

"Works," said Sam. "A Muslim must earn his salvation. Obviously, he must believe in Allah and meet the requirements of the five pillars of Islam. Simultaneously, he must work off his demerits, I mean offset his bad deeds with good deeds."

Rick asked, "Do the doctrines of Islam envision an intercessor advocating forgiveness for one's moral weaknesses before Allah, as Christ does in Christianity?"

"Absolutely not," said George, "and to top it off, a Muslim is not guaranteed forgiveness and eternal life as long as he is upon earth. All their mistakes are only forgiven after death and are totally dependent on Allah's arbitrary will."[2]

"My gosh," said Rick. "That means that a Muslim must spend his whole life in fear, not knowing whether the things he does will be sufficient for eternal life. Allah sure has made it tough on his people. It is obvious why death as Allah's warrior on the battlefield plays such a key role in Islamic doctrine."

"Yes," responded George. "The other incentive for the warrior is paradise offers the company of beautiful virgins and wonderful surroundings. To me, the emphasis appears to be on a carnal heaven where meeting human physical needs, including sex, is highlighted more than the spiritual aspects of eternity."

"I guess everyone has heard about this aspect of Islamic paradise," said Rick. "I am dumfounded as to how Muslims can accept this doctrine while castigating the West for inappropriate morals as part of their anti-West ravings. The Islamic doctrine seems to imply one should live an exemplary moral life on earth because Allah will sanction your immoral life in eternity. I do not understand this paradox. Nor do I understand why we in the West are so timid about addressing this aspect of the Islamic faith and politics."

Sam said, "I think the answer is most people aren't focused on religion, while multiculturalism and political correctness provide a sense of intimidation, causing them to be hesitant about challenging any aspect of Islam. Remember yesterday, we talked about dhimmitude in Europe. Well, this is another example of it in our own country."

"Based on what's happening there, you'd think we'd get the message," said Rick. "We certainly are seeing many more authors warning us about Islamic dangers."

"That is true, but what are our federal agencies doing to educate us? Even the FBI uses 'cultural experts' to sensitize its agents. If I was a Muslim with a jihadist bent, I know what I would be telling them about Muslims. I'd be doing everything I could to nullify any actions against the faithful, wouldn't you?" offered Sam.

"Sorry guys," Rick said. "I need a break ... be right back. You've succeeded in challenging my computer, and there is still more to go. Can't I just go to sleep with earphones or something to absorb all this by osmosis? It would make it so much easier."

"We understand, but this is more fun. We get to see you squirm as your seat gets numb and to observe the light bulbs going off as you catch the true significance of what is being said. Oh no!" Sam chuckled with a smile. "This is more fun. Ha! Ha!"

After returning, Rick found Sam and George in the kitchen, with George telling Sam some of the story about Mark. As Rick approached the two, Sam said, "Rick, you never told me about Mark. Sounds as if he is quite a guy."

"He is, Sam, and I think you'll enjoy meeting him."

George picked up his Coke and headed back to the study, with Sam and Rick in tow. When they were comfortable again, he said he had just a couple more things he wanted to go over before they ended the day.

George opened by saying that he feared their discussion of jihad had been too limited. He wanted Rick to understand the totality of this concept as it was taught and used by Islam. With that thought in mind, he asked, "Rick, have you run across the term 'civilizational war' in any of your readings or discussions?"

"Yes, it seems to me a book entitled something like *The Clash of Civilizations*, or something to that effect, came out recently."

"Good, Rick, I am glad you are aware of Samuel Huntington's book. I am sure you know his thesis centered on the post-cold war global era and the clash of civilizations due to ethnic and religious global tensions."

"I have heard the theory, George, but I understand this is a disputed concept."

"I have to agree with you, Rick, but to my way of thinking, jihad is a civilizational war. There are two reasons for saying this. First, jihad uses every aspect of civilization as an element in war. Violence, education, fear, psychology, sociology, population, immigration, public relations, corruption, and religion all are used in jihad. Military force and terror are the smallest part of jihad. Second, the purpose of jihad is to annihilate every aspect of the non-Islamic civilization. Art, history, law, dress, manners, names, education, customs, government, foreign policy, economics, and every other detail must be made Islamic."[3]

Rick interrupted, "George, I understand total submission is the desired result. For the captive, the choices are few: become Muslims, leave, or pay taxes. In the process of getting to this point, the jihadist uses every aspect of the culture under attack against itself. For example, it's becoming clearer to me that our freedoms are being used against us today, particularly the openness of our society. While incidents of violence such as torture, rape, and murder, along with the annihilation of families and complete communities, have taken place in Europe recently, it seems more likely to me that intimidation, rumor, gossip, blackmail, fraud, favoritism, and deception will be used against us initially."

"Rick, when the goal is the total annihilation of an existing culture so that it remains Islamic for the rest of time, you can be assured every technique we have discussed, along with many we haven't, will be used by the jihadist."

Sam jumped into the discussion to highlight the fact that fear is the driving force behind total subjugation.

George said, "That's true. And you must understand, doctrinally all Muslims must play a part in jihad if they desire to remain Muslims and stay in Allah's good grace. Money is always a big issue, and the Koran leaves no doubt that if you are not fighting, you should be supporting the fighters with your resources. But there are also many other ways to support jihad: proselytizing, assisting in the development of Islamic organizations, community organizing, building voting blocs, fighting for acceptance of Islamic religious favoritism in society, and getting Muslims positioned in elected and nonelected offices of government. Eventually, if history repeats itself, your dhimmi status allows you only to be free in your own home. Outside, it would be an Islamic world where you walk on eggshells. No matter where you go, you would be subject to the whims of any Muslim, good or bad."[4]

Rick said he was sure there were many who would say such a scenario was impossible, but in Europe today, you see this in the Muslim enclaves of major cities. Of course, in terms of witnessing a total jihad in recent years, he suspected the suppression of the Afghani people by the Taliban fit this bill. "Even here, though," he said, "we are talking about Muslim versus Muslim. Nevertheless, their acts of violence and submission techniques seem to cover the whole spectrum you've mentioned."

Sam added, "Yes, and immigration has played a significant role in Europe. Today, Muslims are close to 20 percent of the population across the continent. The results are obvious, as Rick stated. Europeans are being forced out of Muslim enclaves, and the Muslims are demanding more and more special privileges. This is a typical tactic ... replace your culture with aspects of Islam and eventually Islam dominates."

George went on, "In the States, we read of Muslims wanting special education sessions for public school students, special prayer rooms, special ablution areas, new Islamic schools, new mosques, the development of Islamic organizations seeking a greater voice in society than their numbers would justify, special privileges in dress, and the observance of Islamic religious dictums alien to our civil laws. The fact that our citizens grant any of these requests illustrates a lack of understanding of Islamic political goals and tactics. It also means a gradual and ever-increasing surrender to dhimmitude."

George took a breath and continued, "We have talked about the political duality between Islam and kafirs, and you've heard a little about the personal duality between the Muslim and the non-Muslim. While it has been mentioned earlier, the greatest duality internal to Islam is between men and women. You have seen this played out in public because of the dress modern imams proscribe for women. What you probably do not know is that twenty years ago, this style of attire was just beginning to come back into vogue. In fact, only the orthodox women in the Middle East veiled back in the sixties and seventies. Most Middle Eastern women appeared in public dressed as Western women today. The resurgence of political Islam has been a big factor in bringing this attire back into the public mainstream."

"I have trouble with this," said Sam. "This attire always signals that political Islam is alive and well wherever I see it in public. The jihadists use it to send a signal of their presence and growth in a community and country. Local non-Muslim inhabitants become more fearful and submissive as the Islamic numbers increase in a community. Without a doubt, it is also used by jihadists to control fellow Muslims because the doctrines of Islam are on the jihadists' side. Therefore, if you want to show you are a good Muslim, you insure your women are properly dressed."

"We are all aware that Islam supports a male world and demands submission of its women," said George. "Equality in any form doesn't exist; beatings are authorized in the Koran. Mohammad said hell was filled with women, their inheritance rights are half of a man's, and menstruation makes them unclean and restricts their activities. That's not all; it takes two women to counter the testimony of a man in court, they cannot go out of the house unless accompanied by a male, and in divorce, custody belongs to the father with visitation rights to the mother. There is much more, and it is worth reading about Islam's dictums for women."

"You left out the biggest one: polygamy," said Rick. "We have it in the States today. I am sure there are many young men willing to accept such a delightful concept if it became legal, until they actually had more than one wife. But it has survived in the Muslim world down through the centuries and could act as an incentive for some collaboration with the Islamic community in achieving their goals. Now don't misunderstand, I am not advocating polygamy. Everyone knows it plays havoc with the family, but I think there are those in our society who would buy into it today if given the chance."

"You're probably right, Rick," Sam said. "Frankly, my hope is Islam never gains enough footing in the United States to foster these concepts in our society, and if it does, I pray our women will lead the charge against it. But I am not too sure. In visiting the local mosque, a former Christian woman was used to acquaint the visitors with Islam and its wonderful attributes. I would love to go back and see how she is doing in a few years. One thing for sure, I do not believe our wives will stand for such treatment. Even so, government can impose laws and rulings you may not like, and you may not have any opportunity to influence them. Think about some of the issues judges have ruled upon in the last few years."

"I see that our time is running out, Rick," George said. "Let me simply summarize some points that might be important to you later. There is absolutely no historical example of harmonious living between Christianity and Islam. Islam's greatest strength is its ability to divide and confuse the kafirs."[5]

Rick offered, "Dividing and confusing the West is certainly evident in the world today. Most blame the division and confusion on U.S. policies and the economic status of the world, particularly regarding oil. My experience tells me that Islamic governments and their petro dollar-stuffed coffers are playing more havoc in international political, cultural, and economic affairs than most Americans appreciate. We are asleep, while Islam is at war with us. Their leaders certainly have expressed their goals and ambitions often enough. I'm afraid our greed gets in the way of our best interests, and this is one of the ways in which Americans and others in the West wind up being collaborators. Give them the money, and they inadvertently, or intentionally, sell to the highest bidder without truly investigating the end results. I definitely believe we need a strong Homeland Security filled with patriotic individuals who won't compromise our country for any reason."

"We both agree with you, Rick," said Sam.

"In summary," George said, "I'd just like to make a few points worth remembering, Rick. I've watched you take good notes, but you just might like to write these twelve points down. They could be helpful during your reviews of our discussions:

1. War usually consists of two elements: killing and propaganda. Islam has no equal in its war of propaganda.
2. Over half of the Koran is about kafirs.
3. The doctrine of Islam is kept difficult to understand by those who want to retain their prestige and power.

4. Always talk to Muslims based on the doctrine of Islam because the doctrine of Islam is the only real Islam.

5. Duality is the key to every aspect of Islam.

6. There is no Golden Rule in Islam.

7. Both Islamic ethics and logic are subject to duality.

8. The eternal goal of Islam is complete dominance.

9. The differences in Islam are religious not political.

10. The largest growth in Islam is based on birth rates, not conversions.

11. The use of *taqiyya*, or deception, is available to all Muslims without Allah's penalty.

12. There must be collaboration for Islam to succeed, and above all, a Muslim may reform, but Islam cannot.[6]

"Well, Rick," George said, "that's it for me! I hope I have been able to add a little to your knowledge, or at least spark your interest in areas of further investigation. Please do not hesitate to call me any time you have a question. I'm always available to help someone who seeks the truth. By the way, I would like to receive copies of your different articles if you think about it."

With that, the three of them got up and headed for the door. George had to get home and collect his family for supper. Sam had offered to pick up Mark on their way to the Shatilas, and this would take a little more time than normal. Everyone was ready to relax.

CHAPTER 16
Beirut Alumni Evening

By five, everyone at the Flynns' was ready to go. The drive to Mark's at the Base BOQ was slowed by traffic, but it gave the three of them time to review the activities of the past two days. Rick had had a lot thrown at him; he was tired but very pleased. There was no question their discussions had been very beneficial in terms of his knowledge and future writing projects.

It took about thirty minutes to get to Mark's. He was waiting, and although they had much to talk about, Rick sped him out the door and into the car, where he introduced him to Sam and Trudy.

Dressed in a sports jacket and tie, Mark was a handsome guy. About six feet tall, the observer could see he was an athlete. His blond hair accentuated his tan, square-jawed face. He liked to smile, and his smile lines seemed to be permanently etched into his facial features. As the conversation rambled aimlessly on their trip to the Shatilas, both Trudy and Sam decided they really liked him. Rick had known they would, because Mark was a natural-born likable guy who had great self-confidence, and his casualness made others feel comfortable in his presence.

As they pulled up to the door, Sam said this would probably be a new experience for Mark since most of the attendees were graduates of the Beirut Universities. Mark replied he'd heard a lot about Lebanon and was sincerely interested in learning more if he could, especially the food. Sam laughed and told him not to hesitate to ask about anything. While everyone spoke English, he warned Rick and Mark the accents could be a little heavy and their idioms unclear at times but not to let that trouble them. Most of them were great folks, and he thought he'd really enjoy their company.

Trudy, Rick, and Mark headed for the door while Sam parked the car. He'd told them not to wait, as he'd be along shortly. Trudy did the honors when Samir opened the door. Daud was right behind him, and her introduction followed quickly. Without waiting for Sam, she moved slowly into the family room, with her entourage following. The doorbell rang again and Samir went to answer. Sam joined them in a few minutes, and he and Trudy began moving slowly through the group so Rick and Mark could meet everyone.

Trudy saw George, Najwa, and Hannah sitting off to the side, talking to Abe and Cynthia. She had a twinkle in her eye as she maneuvered the group in that direction. Sam could guess what she had on her mind. He chuckled to himself and dutifully followed her. Rick, Sam, and Trudy watched carefully as Mark was introduced to Hannah. Perceptions can be misleading, but it seemed that he raised his eyebrows as the wolf in him reacted to her attractiveness. Rick thought, *"Oh boy, Ann's missing a good show."*

Everyone had a drink. The conversation was light, and the Lebanese hors d'oeuvres absolutely outstanding. Mark and Rick talked a little about old times but George told them both to sit down a minute and let the family know about their careers. Mark said he was currently an aerial refueling pilot at the base who had seen the world as a pilot from 30,000 feet. He was born in Havre, Montana, along the Milk River. However, because of his dad's work, he lived most of his life in Atlanta.

Rick said he couldn't compete with that as he'd spent a little time in the Army and was currently a teacher and free-lance writer, with most of his articles focusing on aspects of the War on Terror since 2001.

Hannah asked if they'd known one another long. Mark replied, "Since 1991 in Iraq."

She said, "It seems odd to me that you two would meet under such circumstances, unless you were in a headquarters someplace."

"That's right," said Mark. "I was a forward air controller charged with identifying targets on the ground and helping pilots to spot them if it was needed. At the time, I was a fighter pilot. After the war, I decided I'd rather slow down a bit so I applied for KC-135's. I was surprised when I was selected, but have no complaints."

Just then, a young Lebanese doctor by the name of Mahmoud Tariq approached the group and introduced himself to the newcomers. It was obvious that everyone knew him. As the conversation ensued, they discovered he was a Palestinian who trained in Beirut and went on to do his pediatric residency at Boston University. He was also the doctor for Hannah's children and a number of other families in the group.

He asked Hannah, "Has Thomas gotten over his cold?"

She responded, "Yes, the kids are fine. How have you been?"

"As you know, I've been in Germany. The work you pile on my desk has kept me tied up and worn me out ever since." Everyone laughed.

Mark said, "Where have you been going in Germany? I've spent some time there."

"To visit my brother in a small town outside Frankfurt."

George said, "I thought he was still in Lebanon."

"No, he moved there several years ago and we are close."

"Well, the paperwork can wait," said Hannah. "It is nice that you can get away to see him. I envy you the opportunities but I am not sure I'd enjoy all those flights. I hope he isn't sick."

"No, we have some joint business ventures and we need to consult periodically."

Supper was announced and the ladies rose to go through the buffet line. They returned to where they had been sitting. The men followed them through the line. George nudged Mark to the lead and indicated he should sit next to Hannah. Mark didn't have a problem with this idea, he liked it very much, and it didn't take very long for the two of them to get into an animated conversation. Trudy noticed that they seemed to be very comfortable together. Neither of them got up when dessert was announced. Only the invitation to coffee seemed to jar them out of their discussion. Mark did the honors. While he was gone, Mahmoud slipped into his chair and asked Hannah if she would be available for dinner one night the coming week? As Mark returned, he overheard Hannah say, "Yes, I will be."

Mahmoud remarked, "We'll talk Monday." Hesitating, he surrendered the chair to Mark.

It was time for the guest speaker to say a few words. Samir introduced him as Abdul Rahman, a friend who'd come from Palestine recently and was traveling around the country, visiting family while updating friendly groups on the Middle East. He thanked him for being with the group this evening and sat down.

Abdul started by saying that it was good to be visiting and he enjoyed meeting so many friends of the Middle East. Unfortunately, from this point on, his tone changed and he went into a diatribe against the United States and Israel. From his perspective, the situation in the Occupied Territories remained very unstable in the face of U.S. and Israeli intransigence. There was talk of putting a wall up to separate

Palestinians and Israelis, as the suicide bombers had taken a significant toll in Israeli lives and spread much fear throughout the country. He promised there would be no let-up of these activities as there were more than enough Palestinians who would sacrifice themselves as *shaheed*, martyrs, in the name of Allah. The Intifada had proved that, over and over. He railed against our government for its murderous, indiscriminate bombings, and shootings in Iraq and the sectarian violence it had generated.

He was sure the only reason we were there was for the oil and occupation of the country in the face of a total lack of regional support. He was certain our presence was stimulating Iranian transgressions, and he feared an expansion of the war to achieve our goals. He referred to Bush as another Hitler and warmonger, who was marching to his own drum and not that of the American people. He praised the disunity in our country. He was particularly elated about the disunity between the United States and our former European allies. Bush's cowboy image throughout the world seemed to be adding credence to the Palestinian position, and many of these European countries had come to the side of Palestine. He praised Hamas for its humanitarian and social work and downplayed its militant operations as totally defensive in nature. He predicted nothing but a continuance of the same type actions until Israel was brought to its knees and annihilated. With a polite thank you to the group for being able to address them, he asked if anyone had questions or comments.

Rick and Mark had been listening and observing the reaction of the group as Abdul spoke. In a mixed group of Arab Christians and Muslims under such circumstances, there could always be some tension, and Abdul's remarks had raised the hackles of many who loved the United States for what it stood for and their ability to take advantage of our freedoms to improve their lives. They all knew such opportunities were not available to the same extent in their home countries. While the Muslims among them delighted in accepting the same freedoms, they had been taught that Islam, not a secular United States, received first priority. Thus, there were a number who showed open and gleeful acceptance of Abdul's message, while others sat in stunned silence, hardly able to believe his words.

One of Mahmoud's friends, Dr. Abid Soussa, exhibited the telltale signs of agreement with Abdul and a number of others. He said that Hamas had provided assistance to his family members in Gaza, and he asked the group to consider sending financial support to help against the repressive tactics of the Israelis. A couple others agreed with him and proceeded to discuss how best to get money to them.

At this point, Abdul said he wanted to ask the group to take up the support of the Palestinian cause as they interacted with other Americans. From his perspective, it was important to tell the truth about the cause to as many Americans as would listen. Perhaps over time, many could be swayed to agree that American policy needed to be changed. In any case, he asked they do all they could.

Sam's group remained silent. It was obvious Samir was uncomfortable. They were not about to get into an argument with Abdul, and they did not want to do anything that would generate or intensify the existing group dynamics. On the other hand, they were all taken aback that this man would come into this country and talk so adversely about its president and foreign policy. Most of them wanted to take him outside and have a go, but they all knew it would do no good. However, monitoring Abdul's activities suddenly became a little more important to George, and they all suspected he would make the FBI aware of what happened here this evening. Then, quietly and subtly, appropriate countermeasures could be employed to make sure he didn't get too far out of line. Individually and as a group, all thought the best solution was deportation, but he might be beneficial in leading them to others of like mind who were more dangerous.

When the question-and-answer period was over and the affair was breaking up, Mahmoud and Abid sauntered over to Hannah.

Mahmoud said, "Well, what do you think?"

Hannah simply looked at him and said she was certainly glad that she was a citizen of the United States.

He responded, "Yes, we all are."

Abid couldn't resist saying, "Aren't you proud of the Palestinians and their defiance of the Israelis?"

Just then, Mark stepped up to them and told Hannah that George and Najwa were ready to depart.

Mahmoud nodded his head and Abid frowned, saying, "Good evening" as they walked away.

Mark held out his arm for Hannah, and the two of them headed for their hosts, thanked them, and proceeded to George's car. As Mark helped Hannah into the car, he said, "Would you be available for supper tomorrow evening?"

Hannah thought for a second and said, "Yes. Why don't you pick me up about six and meet my children before we head to supper?"

Mark smiled a little nervously. The thought of children reminded him of all the women with kids he'd dated in the past … nothing ever seemed to work out … he didn't know if it was his fault, the kids, or their mother's. Nevertheless, he wasn't going to spoil the opportunity to be with this attractive woman, so he responded, "That'd be great, I'd love to meet them. Tomorrow night, I can show you all of Tampa from the top of the Marriot."

"As strange as it might be, I have never been there before. See you at six."

When he was settled in Sam's car, Trudy said, "Did everyone enjoy their evening?" Nodding heads indicated they had.

Rick asked, "What did you think about the speaker?"

Sam coughed a bit before saying, "I didn't care for his presentation, and Samir was more uncomfortable then I'd ever seen him that Abdul would speak the way he did in front of such a mixed Beirut group."

Abe had pulled Sam aside before departing and mentioned to him that Abdul was much worse in his condemnation of the United States when speaking in Arabic. Abe had attended other get-togethers and said you would have thought he was speaking in Palestine, not the United States. Abe also let it be known Abdul did an excellent job of fundraising among the group. Sam said he had informed George, and from his perspective, it was in FBI hands now.

Thinking of Ann, Trudy couldn't help asking Mark, "Did you enjoy meeting Hannah?"

He said, "'Enjoy' isn't the correct word. I loved meeting her … I think I'm in love … and I think I am going to pursue that lady like she has never been pursued before!" Mark's answer stunned everyone into silence for a couple of seconds.

"Well, I'll be darned," said Rick. "After all this time, someone's caught your fancy. Boy! Wait until Ann hears about this!"

They all laughed and joked about Mark's enthusiasm all the way to the BOQ. As they parted, Rick made him promise to keep everyone informed about the success of his courtship. Mark agreed, thanked everyone for a delightful evening, and promised to keep in touch.

As they headed home, Sam said, "Well, that is love at first sight if I ever saw it. Do you think it was reciprocal, Trudy?"

"Well, I am not certain but I do believe there is a lot of interest in that young man. I do not think I have seen Hannah light up like she did tonight at any time since she has been in the States. I sure hope it works out for all of them. I suspect the children will have a lot to do with it in the end. Regardless, I am excited for both of them. They would make a great couple."

Rick commented it had been quite an evening. He said he'd been surprised that such a message had been addressed to this group. He was aware Arabs said one thing to their American acquaintances in English and another to their fellow countrymen in Arabic, but he'd thought they were more cautious than he'd witnessed tonight. Maybe Abdul felt because they were Beirut alumni, they might be more receptive and supportive. In this day and age, it is hard to understand the rationale for such rashness, although it is evident the Palestinian groups have a renewed sense of boldness and freedom about pushing their propaganda harder than in the past. Arab and Iranian oil money has helped, but the Europeans have been pretty negative in their approach to Israel individually and at the U.N. Rick said that such signals sent the wrong message to Palestinian jihadists.

"I agree, Rick," Sam said, "but the thing that bothers me about tonight is it could be the beginning of the end of our Alumni Group. These issues are very divisive and allowing such presentations to occur opens an uncomfortable can of worms for all the membership. We should be reminding ourselves of the great college days we experienced instead of trying to turn our association into a political rally. Such foolishness can only lead to trouble. I told this to the president of the group this evening; however, it may already be too late. My perception is he made a big mistake. I hope I am wrong. I like the people, the jokes, the things we share in common, and the food. I'd hate to see it disappear."

As Sam pulled the car into the garage, both Rick and Trudy agreed this evening was not a good one from that perspective.

Before heading upstairs, Sam asked Rick if he would like to join them for church and lunch tomorrow. Rick nodded and asked if Sam could get him to the airport after lunch, as his departure was at three and he needed to be at the airport a couple of hours early. Sam said that sounded like a good plan to him, and they all headed off to bed.

CHAPTER 17

First Date

Mark arrived in front of Hannah's about five minutes to six in his Mercedes sports car. He'd been a little nervous all day. He didn't want anything to go wrong tonight. His attraction to this Lebanese beauty was strong. On the other hand, he didn't know much about the Lebanese, and he knew Rick's friends wouldn't appreciate any mistakes on his part. Such thoughts bounced around in his head all day. To be sure, nothing would be gained by being late. He'd been meticulous in his planning, and everything was on track as he pulled up to Hannah's home. Getting out of the car, he grabbed the flowers he'd picked up around the corner. They were an important little gesture learned from his past dating experiences. His mind was made up. He was going to do everything possible to attract this lady's attention.

As he rang the doorbell, he said to he prayed silently, "Okay, Father, help me handle this evening right."

It was Jacqueline who opened the door. He said, "Hi! I'm Mark Fields. Your mom and I have a dinner date this evening." Holding out the flowers, he said, "These are for the family. I hope you enjoy flowers."

Jacqueline introduced herself and took the flowers at the same time, saying, "Please come in … the family room is to the right … make yourself at home … Mom will be down in a minute." With that, she headed for the kitchen to get a vase.

Mark found himself a comfortable chair and proceeded to survey the room. The furniture was nondescript and tasteful. The pictures, art, and room accessories definitely transported one's thoughts to the Middle East and to happier family times. There were several pictures of Hannah and her husband, as well as group shots with the kids. As might be expected, George and Najwa were prominent in a couple of photos, along with Sam and Trudy. He was sure that Hannah must sit in this chair often. From this vantage point, she could take in all the pictures while allowing her mind to remember the wonders of the days that had faded into memories.

As he was musing about this, Hannah entered the room. She wore a simple black dress with a colorful print overshirt that highlighted her dark hair and hazel eyes. She took his breath away.

With a smile, she said, "Hi, Mark." She came over, shook his hand, and asked, "Where is Jacqueline?"

"I brought some flowers for the family and she headed to the kitchen for a vase."

"That was thoughtful. Did she call Johnny?" Mark shook his head no, as she went on, "I'd like to have you meet him, he loves to watch the planes when we are driving down around the base."

"Sure," said Mark. With that, Hannah called upstairs to Johnny. Shortly, he came bounding down the stairs two at a time. Both he and Jacqueline had their mother's olive complexion, dark hair, and hazel eyes.

As he came into the room, Hannah said, "Thomas, this is Colonel Mark Fields. He is a pilot at MacDill. I thought you might like to meet him."

"Hi ... Colonel Fields. Glad to meet you. I love airplanes. Could you show me yours sometime?"

Hannah rolled her eyes as Johnny gave him a big smile.

They shook hands and Mark told him he was glad to meet him. He went on to say his mom had said he had an interest in flying. He asked, "So you think you might like to visit the base and see some of the aircraft? I think that might be arranged."

Johnny didn't hesitate to give him a big smile and let him know he would be delighted. Mark said, "Okay, I'll talk to your mom and we'll see if we can't set up a day in which you and your sister and your mom and I can have lunch at the officers' club and tour the flight line."

Johnny said simply, "Gee, that would be great!"

Just then, Jacqueline came around the corner with the flowers. She had put them in a lovely vase and arranged them exquisitely; in fact, they looked as if they'd just been delivered from the best florist shop in town.

Mark sighed and said, "Wow! Jacqueline, you did an absolutely fantastic job arranging those flowers. You don't work in a flower shop, do you? Tell you what, when I buy flowers, I'll bring them to you for arranging."

Jacqueline blushed a little, but she was very pleased with Mark's comments. Hannah also had a smile on her face as she said, "Okay you two, we have got to be going. Make sure your homework is ready for tomorrow before you go to bed. I won't be late. You both have my cell phone number if you need me."

As they headed off to do as asked, they told Mark they enjoyed meeting him and looked forward to seeing him again. With that, he and Hannah headed for the car.

As they drove to the Marriot, Mark said that Hannah seemed to have two very special children. "How do they do in school?"

"Fine. We came to the States in 1995 when Jacqueline was four and Johnny was two. They are more American than Lebanese. Dad and Mom thought it would be good to make certain they learned Arabic when they were young so they could interact with the family back home. They understand it better than they speak it. I think it is valuable to have such knowledge."

Marked nodded, letting her know he thought it was great. "They say if a child learns a language before the age of six, he or she will have it for life. I know I picked up some Navajo from some of Dad's farmhands as a kid, and I still remember it. No, I'm not a linguist, but I can carry on a fairly pleasant conversation."

Hannah replied, "You ought to try Arabic."

"Are you offering to teach me?"

"No," she laughed, "but I'll bet Dad could give you a run for your money, if you desire."

"I think I'd better stick to piloting airplanes. I have less chance of doing or saying the wrong thing."

"You're probably right, but if you hang around Sam and Trudy long enough, you may pick up more than you think possible, particularly if you learn to like Lebanese food."

"I really enjoyed the food last night, and I look forward to sampling some more soon."

"Maybe that can be arranged."

Marked pulled the car up to the Marriot. The valet took the keys and they headed to the elevator.

Hannah commented, "You know Mark, we have lived here for ten years and because of the kids and my social situation, I have not ventured far from home. This is a first for me."

"Well, I hope you enjoy it. You'll get to see a lot of the greater Tampa area. It's different and with a wonderful lady for a dinner partner, I cannot think of a better way to spend an evening."

"I'm going to have to watch you, Mark. There's a lot of blarney in that head of yours."

The elevator stopped and the doors opened; the maitre d' greeted them and led them to their table adjacent to the window. It was a beautiful evening, highlighted by a harvest moon and the brilliant skyline of Tampa. It took a while to grasp the beauty, reality, and fantasy of it all as one's mind tried to juggle all three scenarios at once. With the attraction of Hannah sitting across the table from him, the tension in every nerve in his body was heightened and the excitement level almost made him feeble-minded.

The waiter came. Hannah ordered fish, Mark steak; a throwback of their upbringing. Each had a glass of wine and savored the presence of the other as they slowly sipped it and talked.

Hannah said she was curious how a young man from Montana wound up in Atlanta and the Air Force. Mark said he'd been raised on a small ranch in Montana. His dad inherited a large ranch, but was a businessman in the town and really did not have time for the ranch. As a result, his uncle managed the ranch, and Mark and his brothers had spent their free time after school and in the summers doing anything and everything that was needed to keep it going. It was hard, rough-and-tumble work, but you grew up fast.

He said he loved to ride his horse as a teen, the faster the better. To him, there was nothing like the thrill of riding and thundering hell-bent-for-election over the foothills as adrenalin rushed through every part of his body. "I loved that part of it," he said. "But there were limitations. I can remember entering the junior rodeo thinking I was the next champion rider. The result was disastrous. I spent more time flying through the air and landing with a crunch than I care to talk about. I soon gave up on this idea.

"I graduated from high school just as Dad received an offer to buy his business. The company that bought it wanted him to work for them. The catch was they wanted him in Atlanta. It was a big decision for him and Mom, but in the end, they decided spending a few years in a big city might be good for the family. Uncle Jim was doing a great job with the ranch, so off we went to Atlanta."

"That must have been hard for you," said Hannah. "Mom, Dad and I have talked about our move to the States many times. It was pretty hard on all of us initially."

"Well, I suppose there were certain similarities, although the cultural aspect of your move from Lebanon was probably a lot more severe than mine from Montana. I must admit living in the big city is a lot different, and I am not certain I am truly used to it today. There is something about those wide-open spaces, the independence, and sense of freedom you experience in the West that just can't be beat.

"Of course, I was in the process of heading for college, and that always means a break from home, even if you are living with your parents. It was cheaper, yes, but Mom and Dad really took to the big city with all of its entertainment opportunities, so they weren't around too much. I did my best to master everything they threw at me about business, joined a fraternity, and stumbled over some of my priorities concerning school in the process. I did join the Air Force ROTC and was called to active duty upon graduation."

Changing the subject, Mark said, "There are probably a lot of war stories I could tell you, but turnabout is fair play, so tell me about yourself."

"When Sam visited our home in Lebanon, the country was experiencing dynamic change of the worst kind. The majority of people in Lebanon had been Christian and peaceful. Yes, there were tensions as the population began to shift with the influx of Muslim Palestinians, but it was the militant Muslims and their support from neighboring governments that generated the civil war, which eventually turned Lebanon into a majority Muslim country with invasions from both Israel and Syria. I don't want to get into this tonight. We can discuss it some other time.

"On the other hand, you do need some background to understand why Dad and Mom moved us to Beirut. It is an international city, so they thought the presence of foreigners might help stabilize our lives until the internal strife and fighting stopped. We lived there for twenty years, as Dad worked for the embassy, but things never truly got better. So in 1995, the family moved to Tampa and I came with them.

"I was married at twenty-one as I finished up at the university in Beirut. David was a wonderful man who worked in his family's computer business. We met in college. He was a whiz with computers, particularly programming. There were countless opportunities available to him in the Middle East, but he believed he should be in the family business and that meant we needed to stay in Beirut. Family life in the city was enjoyable. At the same time, we were able to spend many hours at the family summer home in the mountains just east of Beirut. Jacqueline was born in 1991 and Johnny in 1993 just before coming to the States.

"David was a robust athletic man who was not afraid of anything or anyone. You probably saw his picture at the house."

"Yes, I did. He had a great smile, and I swear that in one of the pictures, I could see mischievousness in his eyes. Did he have a little imp in him?"

She laughed and said, "He sure did! He was the love of my life, and he had a magnificent capacity to love everyone. Our marriage was truly wonderful.

"The mountains east of Beirut are beautiful and close. Just about all of our friends went there in the summer to beat the heat of the city and relax. One night in late fall of 1994, we had gone up to the family summerhouse just to take a break and get away from David's office. There had been news of small fights between Christians and Muslims throughout Lebanon all summer. None had come even close to us. Because of this, we never expected to be involved in any fighting, thinking locked doors would be sufficient to keep us safe. That was our mistake. Just before dusk one evening, five men approached the house and called for the family to come out. David couldn't believe what he was hearing, because they were obviously Muslims looking for a family to torment. He went to the door and began talking to them through it, telling them to move on and no one would be coming out. The conversation became more and more heated the longer they talked. Suddenly, one of the men outside yelled, '*Allah Huwa Akbar*,' and fired his automatic weapon through the door, killing David in front of me." Her eyes filled with tears as she continued.

Mark interrupted her, saying, "Hannah, you don't have to go on."

She shook her head and said, "It's okay. I would like you to know." Then closing her eyes, she added, "As he slumped to the floor, I ran to him. His blood poured out on the hallway floor. I frantically tried to seal the wounds, but they were too severe. I believe he died almost instantly. I was so angry, frightened, and distraught at the same time, I couldn't think straight. They'd killed my David in the name of Allah and ran away shouting some more curses and vulgarities.

"As you can imagine, I was overcome with grief. Within a few minutes, some other family members ran to us from nearby homes and came to my rescue. From that moment on, all of our lives were turned upside down. Mom and Dad were absolutely wonderful to me. They had already made arrangements to come to the States and insisted that I should come with them. With the situation as unstable as it was in Lebanon, I couldn't resist. To be honest, at this moment in my life, I just didn't know how I could survive without them. Then too, without David, I didn't see how I was going to be able to raise the kids. Of course, I knew their grandparents would be wonderful to have in their lives. So we came with them."

"That is quite a heart-rending story, Hannah ... to find yourself with two toddlers and no husband at such a young age must have been very scary. I can understand why you did what you did."

With that, Mark reached over and gently touched her hand as he said, "From my perspective, I can't tell you how thankful I am that you came. If you hadn't, I never would have had the chance to be talking to you now, and I wouldn't have missed that for anything."

Slowly, he pulled his hand back and said, "Our conversation has gone from light to heavy pretty fast. Thanks for sharing with me. Tell me, do you work?"

"Yes, I do. Do you remember Dr. Mahmoud Tariq, the pediatrician I introduced you to last night?" Mark nodded. "He and his friend Dr. Abid Soussa have a small pediatric clinic in town. Several years ago, after meeting him at the Beirut University functions, he asked me if I would consider being a receptionist in his office. I gave it some thought; the money he offered was good, the kids were getting older; so I decided to take a leap of faith. It is really a part-time job since I work from 8:30

to 3:00 Monday through Friday. Sometimes I go in Saturday morning if things are hectic. Most importantly, it has worked out well and really helped me financially."

"Well, I am glad it has worked out, but I kind of got the impression there might be a little more involved than a business relationship. It seems to me I overheard him say he would talk to you Monday about a dinner engagement this week."

"You did. But he phoned this afternoon to tell me he has been called to Germany to see his family again and he needs me to reschedule all of his appointments in conjunction with Dr. Soussa. Regardless, Mark, Mahmoud is a Muslim. I could not be romantically involved with him. I believe the Bible is right in teaching us not to be unequally yoked. I've seen too many disastrous marriages when such wisdom is not followed. Yes, we have dated a few times as friends. I think he is as lonely as I have been over the years, and he has a kind heart. He has done a tremendous job in treating the children, and they respond to him in ways they don't with others."

"That is wonderful to hear, Hannah."

In the car on the way home, Mark remembered what he had told Johnny about visiting the base. He asked Hannah when the best time might be to take everyone to the base for lunch and to visit the flight line. He also said that she could invite her mom and dad if she desired. She said that because of school, it would probably be better on the weekend. Mark asked about the coming Saturday, and she said it would be fine, and that she would ask her mom and dad if they might like to go along. In any case, a date was set for Saturday.

When they got to the house, he opened her door and offered her his hand, and they walked slowly up the walk. Mark felt a little emboldened, and when he got to the front door he said, "You know, Hannah, this has been a lot of fun, and I don't want to wait until next Saturday to see you again. Would it be possible to have dinner Wednesday or Thursday evening? You know, just some little place where we can talk and get to know one another better."

"Mark, that would be wonderful. What about Thursday? I believe Thomas has a soccer game Wednesday evening, which always makes us late getting home."

"That's fine. I'll plan to pick you up at the same time." With that, he leaned forward and gave her a soft kiss. To his great satisfaction, she did not pull away.

He opened the door for her, said good night, and turned and walked to the car with a light heart and a smile on his face. It had been a terrific evening!

CHAPTER 18
Ahmed

Cynthia had taken Abe to the airport Sunday evening. As they parted, she told Abe she hoped Ahmed would join him on his return journey. She didn't know what was happening in Europe but she sensed that Ahmed needed to be in the States. Abe told her he would try again. They kissed and he disappeared into the crowd.

Early the next morning, Ahmed met him at the airport and they drove to his small apartment on the outskirts of Frankfurt. They had lunch and Abe turned to his brother inquisitively and asked, "Okay, Ahmed, why did you contact me, using our old code signal? It's been so long, I hardly remembered what it meant. It took me a few minutes to remember and realize you wanted a one-on-one."

"Sorry, Abe, but I needed to talk to you in person. Let's take a walk." With that, the two men left the apartment, got in the car, and drove to the Frankfurt Zoo. They parked and began to stroll leisurely through the grounds.

After they had walked for a while, Ahmed found a secluded bench and they sat down. At this point, the small talk turned serious. Ahmed let Abe know he was about worn out from the stress and tension surrounding his life in Germany. Abe knew he was a Christian but remained a Muslim outwardly. His work in Lebanon had required him to walk this tightrope. What he hadn't fully comprehended was that his role-playing had been so important to his life in Germany.

Ahmed said, "I hadn't been here six months before our friends contacted me and asked if I would help them monitor the mosques and certain individuals in the area. They also wanted to use our family business as a cover for some of their activities. You know how much I hate the jihadists, particularly their killing of innocents. I just couldn't refuse. Besides they pay well and I have been able to save for my future in the United States. It must be obvious at this point that I agreed and have been working with them since then."

"Abe, you know the situation in Europe. As immigration has increased, the Muslims have gained more and more control in their new countries of residence. Today, there are many areas where the natives are afraid to go into the Muslim enclaves, not only the average citizen, but more significantly, the police and fire departments. Everything is Muslim. They have simply transplanted their native environments to Europe and begun the process of dominating. Assimilation is a pipe dream of the intellectuals who have already assumed a dhimmi status. Tolerance, civil liberties, and many of the other aspects of democracy are being pushed aside in the name of Islam. There are those predicting an Islamic Europe by the end of the century if not sooner. If we do not do something soon, I am afraid that will happen."

"Sorry, Abe, I am frustrated by the stupidity of the intellectuals and elites. They are the collaborators that are assisting in bringing Europe into the Islamic camp. The Ottomans tried before and were defeated. I am afraid deportation, reduced birth rates, refusal to allow further expansion of mosques, strict control of foreign investment and education, along with forced assimilation, are the only way to turn back the tide; right now, it looks hopeless to me.

"Anyway, over the years, I have focused on three mosques in this area. I have gotten to know the attendees well, and I have even used the business to help with some shipments for the mosque to and from the Middle East. Each has been checked for weapons and other contraband without the knowledge of the mosque. While I have not been an openly vocal militant jihadist, I have quietly and carefully played the role of a jihad supporter. Gradually, this group came to trust me with simple tasks of little consequence, and when new individuals arrived in town, I would be chosen as an escort.

"Over the past year, the mosque has experienced more and more traffic from Afghanistan. Muslims from here will go there and return after spending several months. I have also escorted individuals from Afghanistan who are here to preach in our mosque and tour Germany doing the same thing. In every case, the travel seems to be coordinated through our local group. The folks I am working for believe we have an important Al-Qaeda cell in our midst.

"They knew I desired to go to the States, and so nine months ago, they brought in another operative to work with me and take over when I depart. You can imagine how overjoyed I was when this happened; we have worked very well together.

"Recently, we have noticed a few of the more militant members of our group secreting themselves in different places around Germany for a few days at a time. To the unsuspecting, it appears as if they are on some kind of a Muslim retreat. However, the evidence is beginning to mount that something else may be in the wind. We have even had Muslims from Florida visiting the mosque and accompanying the group on their retreat.

"When I sent you that message, I had escorted an Al-Qaeda representative from Afghanistan to a retreat group in southern Germany. He recognized me from our days in southern Lebanon and proceeded to try and recruit me for active jihadist operations. While he never said anything to confirm our suspicions, the inference of his conversation was that something all Muslims would be proud of was being planned. When I left him, he praised Allah and said he hoped I would follow Allah's divine call on my life. The next day, I took two men from the United States to the same retreat.

"Frankly, Abe, his recognition of me from our old days in Lebanon and his recruitment pitch made me uncomfortable. We did some things back in those days I have regretted. You know these guys will use blackmail, and with his knowledge of my history, that is a distinct possibility if they want greater services from me for their cause. I have no desire to compromise my life at this point. After all these years, I am tired and I've told everyone it is time for me to turn the reins over to my partner. They agreed and I plan on accompanying you back to the States, if you and Cynthia don't mind my barging in on you this way."

Abe said, "Heavens no! We have been looking forward to this day for a long time."

That evening Abe helped Ahmed pack several boxes. In the process, Ahmed received a telephone call informing him his escort services were needed in the morning to pick up an arrival from the United States. He was asked to bring him to the mosque. Abe told Ahmed he would continue to pack and make arrangements to ship his things to his house in Florida.

The next morning, Ahmed was off early, picked up his visitor, and delivered him to the mosque. When they arrived, he noticed most of the assembled group had been there earlier in the year. He gleaned that two were from the States, one from Detroit and the other from Atlanta, while two had arrived from Canada. He'd heard another was due to arrive from the States but someone else was picking him up. As the group moved to a conference room in the mosque, Ahmed headed to his office. He needed to let everyone know something unusual was taking place at the mosque.

What bothered him most was the size and militant nature of the jihadists in this group. He'd never seen so many fighters and planners assembled in this manner, and he knew from past encounters all of them had been trained in Afghanistan. According to the recent mosque rumor mill, Allah was getting an elite group of Al-Qaeda fighters together for a special mission. While Ahmed couldn't put a great deal of credence in such talk, his experience and interaction with the mosque officials told him there was more to the rumors than most knew. In fact, his intuition told him the United States was in for a surprise. It had been four years since 9/11, and it was time for another strike. Such a successful operation would not only reinforce Al-Qaeda's image as an international force but also demonstrate the ineffectiveness of Washington's defensive efforts. The targets were not as important as the psychological impact in keeping everyone on edge. Then, too, many countries that supported U.S. efforts might reconsider their stance in the face of a good propaganda campaign focused on U.S. ineptness in countering Al-Qaeda attacks. Yes, Mohammad had evolved good strategic and tactical plans, as Islam became a force in the Arab world and Mediterranean basin. It was apparent Al-Qaeda leaders were following his philosophies in detail.

About four that afternoon, the shipper came by to pick up the few things Ahmed wanted to accompany him to the States. He had elected to tell only a few of his closest friends he was moving to the United States. Everyone knew his company had an office in Tampa, and he'd made certain they all knew his move was business driven, the more plausible and rational, the better.

That evening, he and Abe shared a quiet supper at a local *gasthaus*. They had an early departure in the morning and decided to get as much sleep as they could.

Everything had gone smoothly in getting to the airport and boarding the plane to New York. Their economy seats were pretty far back in the plane but once airborne, they'd be able to move around pretty freely. In any case, it was going to be a long day, and they hoped to make their connection in New York because Cynthia was planning to pick them up; she didn't need to lose sleep in the process.

About halfway through the flight, Ahmed decided to take a good walk around the plane. As he rounded one of the bulkheads to return to his seat, he saw one of the men he'd recently escorted to a retreat meeting in southern Germany reading a magazine. Fortunately, he was not looking at Ahmed, so he turned around and retraced his steps to his seat. When he got there, he poked Abe and said, "Abe, one of the guys I escorted to a southern retreat a few weeks ago is on this flight. I tried not to let him see me. I think we should follow him when we disembark and see what airline destination he has on the next flight."

Abe concurred in Ahmed's idea. Maybe they could learn something helpful to Homeland Security. They moved cautiously once they disembarked. When they got to the customs area, Ahmed pointed to the man he had identified. Abe stopped cold in his tracks. It was Dr. Mahmoud Tariq from Tampa.

Abe told Ahmed he knew this man and he knew exactly where he was going. They might not be on the same plane, but he was headed to Tampa. Nevertheless, he did not want to make Dr. Tariq aware of his presence right now. He told Ahmed the whole story about Rick's visit to Sam's, his teaching, and meeting Mahmoud at the Beirut University

Alumni function last Saturday evening. He also told Ahmed that George's daughter, Hannah, worked for Mahmoud and might be able to shed some more light on his overseas visits. He was absolutely certain no one in Tampa believed Mahmoud could possibly have anything to do with jihadists. He was a doctor, and his treatment of his patients and friends was above reproach in every respect. With this thought to mull on, they headed to their plane's waiting area, taking seats in the area across from their departure gate to observe approaching passengers in case Mahmoud was on the same plane.

As it turned out, he was not on their flight. Unknown to them, he had met another friend and gone off to talk to him before taking a later flight.

True to her word, Cynthia was waiting with open arms as the two of them picked up their baggage. She was excited to see them both. It had been ten years since they had spent a little time with Ahmed in Germany, and she was full of questions. Right now, both men just needed a good night's rest.

Before they arrived home, Abe was on the phone to George, asking if he and Ahmed could have lunch with him tomorrow. He felt their information needed relaying with some urgency. First they both needed a good night's sleep. Lunch provided just the right opportunity for them. George was a great friend.

Meanwhile, as they had flown home, a message flashed across the Atlantic directed to FBI headquarters in Washington from their German counterpart. Such messages never go directly. Because of the separate missions of the agencies involved, they must pass through the CIA station chief in Bonn to CIA headquarters in Langley before being forwarded to the FBI. In any case, this one was urgent and highly classified. It stated that an undercover German agent in Frankfurt had been murdered while investigating several men at a local mosque who were suspected jihadists from Al-Qaeda. In the agent's last report, he stated each of these Al-Qaeda men had traveled extensively in the Middle East and been in Afghanistan several times. All had been involved in so-called retreats in southern Germany that were believed to be terrorist operational planning and training sessions. Any of them could pass for an American businessman because of their very good English. More importantly, in the past six months a number of Americans had repeatedly shown up at the same mosque in Frankfurt. They too had traveled to the retreat sites in the south to join the men reportedly trained in Afghanistan along with individuals from other countries. On one flight, a German agent returning home from a vacation in the States sat next to a Dr. Mahmoud from Tampa, who was later seen in the mosque. With the murder of one of their best agents, German intelligence analysts were certain an Al-Qaeda operation was close to being executed in the United States. The Stateside departure and return cities of those men under surveillance coming to Germany were Detroit, Atlanta, and Tampa. Thus, the Germans believed there was a high probability the targets were located in one, if not all, of these cities. The message closed with a simple statement that observations were continuing. It also wished the FBI well in its quest to uncover the plotters.

CHAPTER 19

Thursday

After breakfast, Sam checked his E-mail. There was a message from Rick saying that he was being recalled to active duty sooner than expected. He asked if he could bring Ann down to help him look for a house over the following weekend. He also commented that he had submitted an article on political Islam. Apparently, his editor was a little leery of publishing it because it didn't give any consideration to the political correctness syndrome that seemed to be so prevalent right now. As a result, he wasn't certain it would be published, but he'd decided to tackle an article on the Muslim Brotherhood as a follow-on to his current piece. He thought he might be able to do a little research for it during his visit and asked if Sam had any good leads. In any case, all of his investigations would pay big dividends when he returned to active duty.

Trudy was elated when she heard the news and told Sam to tell Rick he and Ann could stay as long as they needed. Sam answered Rick with this information and went on to say he was sorry about Rick's conflict with his editor; that was the price one paid for writing anything about Islam that didn't toe the political correctness line. He also commented he had done some research on the Brotherhood, and he was certain both George and Abe would be able to fill in a lot of gaps. He suggested a visit to the local mosque might be appropriate as they permitted Elderhostel educational opportunity visits and would probably welcome his inquiries. He closed by saying that Abe had been due back yesterday but he hadn't had a chance to catch up with him. Sam knew Rick would be curious.

Abe and Ahmed met George at the Valencia in downtown Tampa at noon. George was delighted to see Ahmed again after so many years. There was a lot of catching up to do but Abe was anxious to get to the purpose for their visit. After getting a few "do you remember" exchanges out of the way, Abe told George that Ahmed needed to pass on the information he had acquired. Ahmed explained his work in Europe and his perception that an operation was being planned against the United States in the very near future.

As he finished, Abe told George one of the men Ahmed had escorted to the retreats in Germany was on the plane with them on their return flight. It was Mahmoud Tariq! George didn't show any emotion, but Abe could tell he was surprised, as his eyebrows were raised for a split second.

Ahmed said he was positive there would be others in the area working with Mahmoud and he planned to attend the local mosque services tomorrow in the hopes of identifying them.

George said, "Are you sure it is Mahmoud? That doesn't fit what I know of him. I just don't believe he could be a member of the militant part of the Brotherhood or Al-Qaeda."

Ahmed said he would keep a very low profile and just observe. George added that he would speak to Hannah about Mahmoud's activities and asked Ahmed to call him after his mosque visit. With sincerity in his voice and a concerned look in his eyes, he told Ahmed he would not have to maintain his cover as a Muslim much longer and thanked him for his years of service in Germany and Lebanon. With that, they separated: George to his office while Ahmed and Abe headed home to do some unpacking and begin apartment hunting for Ahmed.

After lunch, George met with his boss, Bud Parker, the Agent in Charge, to discuss Ahmed's information. Bud listened intently and really perked up when George told him about Mahmoud.

"So Ahmed has positively identified Mahmoud as one of the suspected conspirators, and he lives here in Tampa?" said Bud.

"Yes," responded George, "and his story to everyone about traveling to see his family wasn't true because Ahmed confirmed he was at the mosque and on the retreats when in Germany."

"George, I do not believe you have seen the message we received from Germany through Washington, but it tends to substantiate the fact that we may have a problem brewing in Tampa. Not only that, but a CIA report we just received states a couple of men believed to be jihadists at Ahmed's former mosque have disappeared. They also verified Ahmed's suspicion of a possible strike in the United States. It seems Ahmed's former mosque partner told the authorities that the two men in question had shaved their beards and purchased business attire two days before they disappeared. The authorities were in the process of checking all passengers to the States. Unfortunately, it is highly probable they are traveling under assumed names.

"George," Bud continued, "Ahmed could be the key to bringing this group down before anything really terrible happens. I would love to wire him up and send him into that den of vipers, but I don't have enough evidence to support a Foreign Intelligence Surveillance Act (FISA) electronic surveillance request to the Justice Department. If those guys don't have what they consider to be a slam-dunk case, they tend to shy away from granting any physical or electronic surveillance approval. While the pieces of the puzzle are still falling into place, the big nuggets that will get us approval haven't been uncovered yet. When the time comes, do you think Ahmed will be willing to wire-up for us and be a cooperative witness against these guys?"

"Based on his dislike of jihadists, my answer is yes, Bud, but he's been playing these games a long time and wants to return to a normal life."

"Call him," Bud said.

George was able to get right through to Ahmed and after a short conversation, he came back with the message, "Ahmed said he'd be glad to help, but he does not want this to be a habit."

Bud laughed and said, "Okay. That's settled, the minute we have sufficient probable cause from our perspective, we need to fire off an immediate request for both physical and electronic surveillance of these jokers. We also need to alert the U.S. Attorney's Office in Tampa as to what may be going down. We need to get the authorizations quickly if this situation begins to move faster than we now suspect. I don't want to wind up critiquing a crisis that never should have happened. My constant fear is that the probable cause we must have and the request process will lag behind our need to act. I'll brief our squads. Will you make arrangements to get Ahmed here so I can talk to him? I want to make certain he understands his role and the legal issues involved."

With that, George called Ahmed back and said, "Ahmed, Bud wants to speak to you this afternoon. I am sending an agent to pick you up."

Ahmed agreed.

In the meantime, George called his daughter. He knew she would be working late because things always got backed up at the office when Mahmoud was away. He asked if she might be available for a coffee break around three. He said he'd stop by and pick her up. He had often done this in the past, as there was a Starbucks around the corner. He picked her up on time and after getting their coffee, he asked her how the day was going. She responded with a tired shrug and a comment to the effect everyone was playing catch-up. Abid was tense because of the workload, and Mahmoud was rushed but seemed to be his old self. She said she did not know how he did it. Between the telephone calls, crying children, and appointment changes, she was a little stressed out and glad he called.

George said, "I kind of anticipated you'd be having a rough day and I thought a quiet cup of coffee might help before you return to the hustle and bustle of the office. You do have to go back, don't you?"

"Oh, yes."

"Aside from Mahmoud's recent absence, have you noticed anything different about him, Abid, or their friends?"

"No, Dad, except over the past five months, Mahmoud has made a monthly trip to Germany to see members of his family. Abid has had a couple former friends from Syria visit him after hours at the office twice. I had to tidy up after them the next day. I think he hired them to get the storage shed behind the office building cleaned out. There was some talk about the doctors using it for their cars. Otherwise, I can't think of anything."

"Is the garage used for office supply storage?"

"No, our supplies are kept in a small storage closet in the main building. I never have a need to go to the garage, only the doctors have keys anyway. What is all this about, Dad?"

"You've heard me speak of Abe's brother Ahmed in Germany. Well, Ahmed returned with Abe and will be living here; however, on the plane yesterday, he saw Mahmoud and told Abe he was one of the men who met periodically with some of the suspicious militants from one of the Frankfurt mosques."

"No, Dad! Not Mahmoud! I do not see how he could possibly be connected with such men. His personality, character, and life in our community provide no credence to such an accusation. I cannot believe it! It is simply impossible!"

"That was pretty much my reaction as well, but then I got to thinking … it always seems to be the smart ones who lead the cause. My experience and reading indicate that historically, it has been the intellectuals and elites within Muslim society who are providing the philosophical ingredients for our current problems. It is true a few of them actually dirty their hands by acting as suicide bombers, but they provide the incentive for doing so. On the other hand, you do not take a field hand or shepherd and put them at the controls of a modern jetliner to destroy buildings in New York. No, it takes an intelligent person who is dedicated to the Medina portion of the Koran and Allah to do that effectively. The bottom line is doctors having such beliefs can be as deadly in seeking martyrdom as anyone else.

"Another point I need to make is that the Muslim Brotherhood operates overtly and covertly. What we have learned is that individuals who play the overt role are like Mahmoud. They do everything to disarm any concern you might have against the advance of Islam. They can use deceit, misdirection, disinformation, and actual lies if that satisfies their goal. Allah completely absolves them of any wrongdoing. It's in the Koran."

"I know, Dad, but Mahmoud is such a perfect citizen."

"That is the point, he blends with our society while working behind our backs to destroy everything we hold dear."

"I'm sorry, Dad, but I just can't believe he is such a person."

"Okay, okay, but would you pay closer attention to what is going on around you and be careful? If he is playing with fire, I do not want you to get burned."

George took Hannah back to the office, as he always did. The game had changed, but he needed Hannah to act naturally as if she didn't know what had just occurred. As he drove, his cell phone rang. It was Sam. He brought George up to date about Rick and told him Rick would be back in town the weekend after next. George's mind was going a mile a minute, trying to put the pieces of the Mahmoud puzzle together. Sam said he had told Rick he and Abe might be good ones to educate him about the Brotherhood. George said he would be glad to add whatever he could but he'd have to talk later. Sam thanked him and hung up.

As Hannah returned to the office, her perception of Mahmoud was tarnished but not changed. Nothing seemed out of order, and it wasn't long before she thought all her father told her was a big misunderstanding. She didn't give it much more thought and continued her normal activities.

The next time she looked at the clock, she barely had enough time to get home and wash up before the front doorbell rang. Johnny rushed to answer it, knowing his new friend would be there to pick up his mom. He couldn't wait to see him and confirm their trip to the base Saturday. He opened the door with a big smile on his face and said, "Good evening, Colonel Fields!"

Mark chuckled as he shook his hand and responded, "Good evening, Johnny, are you ready for our field trip Saturday?"

"I sure am," he said enthusiastically. "I can't wait. I'll be one of the only kids at school who has been inside one of those monster planes. Do you think you could come to school and talk to our class if the teacher gives me permission?"

Hannah overheard his question as she approached. "Hold on a minute, don't you think you are getting a little ahead of yourself? You haven't even gone to the base yet."

Mark injected, "Johnny, if you get your teacher's permission and your mom doesn't object, I'll be glad to come to your school and speak. Not only that, but if you enjoy your trip Saturday, I'll even ask if I can give your whole class a tour later. What do you think of that?"

"Wow! That would be cool!"

Both Hannah and Mark laughed as he ran off at his mother's direction to do his homework.

Hannah commented, "You sure know how to please a young man. That was a wonderful thing to do."

Mark said, "And what do I have to do to please his mother? That is really my objective in life right now."

"I'm sure you'll come up with something," she said and smiled coquettishly.

She yelled good-bye to the kids and they headed to the car.

Mark said there used to be a favorite little restaurant in Carrollwood called Basel's having exquisite French cuisine but it had closed and he had not found a replacement. On the other hand, the Melting Pot had good fondue and it was a leisurely way to enjoy one's supper companion, so he headed there.

When they were seated and had ordered supper, Hannah apologized for being a little frazzled. She acknowledged it had been crazy with Mahmoud out of the office and returning yesterday to a heavy patient load. She didn't go into a lot of details. On top of that, a call from school had informed her Johnny had been in a scuffle at soccer practice. "He is a very good forward and the other kids like to pass him the ball. If he gets it, he'll generally make a goal. Anyway, one of the boys accused him of hogging the ball, called him a rag-head, and one thing led to another. Now they are both going to sit on the bench for several games. Johnny thought the coach was unfair, as the other boy had started it. We had a long talk. I hope we resolved the problem. I must admit I'm not sure."

"It will be all right. Johnny is a good kid, and I am confident he can get over this pretty easily. I'll be glad to talk to him if you wish."

"No, not now. I'd like to see how our discussion is going to work out before anyone else gets involved."

"That's fine. I didn't see Jacqueline this evening. How is she?"

"She is in the typical teenage years, striving to be an adult. That means too much makeup and pushing me to wear the skimpiest clothes possible. I have to watch her like a hawk. Academically, she is a star and I'm proud of her, but she can pull my chain without too much difficulty. Anyway, between everything that is going on at work and the kids' behavior this week, I have been tempted to cancel our Saturday get-together."

"Let's not do that, Hannah. I know things have been a little hectic and dissatisfying but I think the change of pace would do everyone a world of good. I'm really looking forward to our day out with the kids. Since I am very much attracted to their mother, I thought it might be important to get to know them as quickly as I can. If that sounds selfish, it is. I need to take advantage of every opportunity."

"Mark, you know how to get to a gal's heart: food, flowers, and her children. Tie that together with a lot of sweet talk, and you are on the road to success. How many times have you pulled this on an unsuspecting gal?"

"Never. First, I haven't dated many women with children and second, my social life has been very limited. I've had a few dates over the years with the sisters of friends and done a little double dating to help some of my buddies out, but I have never found anyone I felt attracted to enough to consider a long-term arrangement until I met you. I am beginning to think in different terms. I sense you may be experiencing the same feelings. I don't want to rush anything. Actually, I am savoring each moment, and I do not want to do anything to spoil our relationship. It is just too important to me, and I hope you sense the same thing."

"I do, Mark. I am really anxious to know you better. You've convinced me Saturday would be a good thing. Dad and Mom will not be joining us. Dad told me he thinks he will be working and maybe they could all visit some other time."

They continued to linger over their supper and wine for a couple of hours before Mark noted the time and said he'd better get her home. Based on everything that had been said, it looked as if another long day was in the offing, and he had a practice refueling mission to fly with some new members of the squadron in the morning.

At the door, their lips touched again, and although nothing was said by either, the exhilarating sensation of their kiss almost knocked both of them off their feet. Neither had the slightest thought of turning back the clock. Excitement of the wildest kind gripped both of them as they said good night.

CHAPTER 20
Ahmed's Mosque Day

On the way to the mosque, Abe and Ahmed had stopped at the FBI office for last-minute instructions. Bud had warned Ahmed not to do anything foolish, but that seemed kind of silly inasmuch as he was walking into the stomping grounds of supposedly friendly and known Al-Qaeda members. In any case, there was no point in disagreeing so he smiled, said he understood, and headed out the door.

The plan was simple. Ahmed would enter the mosque at noon after Abe dropped him off. He would keep a low profile, and when the service was over, he would call Abe for pickup.

On entering, he returned the greeting of those who greeted him but he did not initiate any conversations. He wanted to observe. He placed himself in the back of the room. Most of the worshipers arrived just before the appropriate prayer time. Initially, he did not see anyone he knew but as his eyes grew accustomed to the interior, he thought he recognized a couple of people from the back of their heads. Periodically, he glanced that way in the hopes he could get more of a profile, but that didn't work. He knew he would have to wait until people were departing if he was going to get an accurate picture.

As the service came to an end, he checked again; this time, making identification was possible. To his surprise, Abid Soussa stood and began talking with Mohammed Faisal and Abdullah Tallel, whom he also knew from the mosque in Frankfurt. Both had changed their appearance by shaving their beards and dressing like American businessmen. They certainly looked prosperous and at home. Ahmed ducked his head and scurried back into the shadows. He wasn't sure he wanted to be noticed at this point. It might be to his advantage to move slowly until he got a better understanding of this mosque, the community, and his FBI contacts. At the same time, gathering better information was critical, and doing it sooner than later did seem to be very important in quelling the speculation and nailing down the facts.

As the crowd thinned, he saw Abid Soussa and his companions coming his way. He tried to move into another alcove, but it was useless. As Abid got close, he nodded and stopped. The quizzical look on his face was replaced by recognition, and he said, "I know you, you were my escort several times when I came to Germany. Let's see, you're Ahmed; what are you doing here?"

Ahmed smiled and said, "You have a good memory. I have moved here. I got tired of those cold German winters. When friends offered to sponsor me, I took the plunge and here I am."

"I'll bet they miss you at the mosque. I am sure you remember Mohammed and Abdullah."

"Of course but I almost didn't recognize them in their Western attire. It's a pretty dramatic change."

"Yes, they've come to help me and some brothers here at the mosque for a few days. We are preparing a special greeting for the people of Tampa, if you know what I mean."

Ahmed smiled and said, "Praise be to God, I am aware of such special parties. They raise Allah's spirits and provide a warm feeling of strength, comradeship, and single-mindedness to all the *ulema* (community of believers). Venturing forward in this way is courageous and tremendously satisfying for the *Ikhwan* who would crush the crusaders."

"Well said, Ahmed! You are more a man after my own heart and those of my brothers here than I realized. Are you working?" said Abid.

"No, I just arrived last week and haven't found a job yet. But my friend has promised me work later."

"Ahmed! Mohammed and Abdullah are helping me straighten up and paint the office garage as well as my partner, Mahmoud Tariq's, home garage. I am certain you remember him. He's visited the mosque in Germany and other areas as much as I. Would you be free to help? I know you and I believe I can trust you. Let me give you my phone number. Please call in the morning if you think you can help. We'll only be working over the weekend. I pay good wages and I thought you might be able to use some extra cash right now."

"Praise God! That is an answer to prayer. You and Allah are so merciful, Abid. I can't thank you enough for the offer. I don't think my friends have anything planned tomorrow. I'll call early to let you know."

Abid said, "Do you have a car?"

"No, I have a friend picking me up when I call him."

"Tell you what. Mohammed, Abdullah, and I are headed to the office garage right now. Why don't you join us? I can show you the garage and where our offices are at the same time."

Ahmed thought for a moment and said, "That would be great. I can call my friend from there." With that, they loaded into Abid's Mercedes and headed to his office.

Upon arrival, Abid pointed to his office building and asked Ahmed, "Would you mind helping us unload some of these file boxes from the trunk into the garage attic?"

Ahmed didn't see how he could refuse and said, "Sure, I'll be glad to help anytime." It didn't take long. Each of them carried two boxes into the attic, one at a time. This was a little more work than Ahmed had contemplated, and each of them were perspiring a little more than they'd intended by the time they finished.

Abid had warned all three of them to handle the boxes carefully. They had chuckled when Mohammed picked up the first box and groaned under its weight.

Abdullah commented, "Mohammed was one of the skinniest, scrawniest, and weakest Saudis I've ever seen come out of the desert." He went on to pacify him, saying that he made up for it with his ferocious spirit and dislike of the enemy. Having watched him work in the past, he was confident Allah had blessed him with the right talents, thereby ensuring his pleasures in paradise next Monday.

Abid frowned.

Mohammed shot back, "Abdullah is only going to make it to paradise on a wing and prayer. On second thought," he said, "I don't think that is enough or even possible. I am sure Abdullah would have to ride on my coattails as I answer Allah's questions on our way through the heavens, otherwise I don't see much hope."

With that, Abid quickly changed the subject, saying, "We have a lot of work to do tomorrow and Sunday because of the schedule change." He also said that Allah would bless Ahmed's presence.

When the last box was in place and everything secured, Ahmed thanked Abid for the ride and his offer of work. He then said, "I'll call in the morning."

With that he walked around to the office to call Abe and, in the process, acquainted himself with the office and staff.

Abe hadn't been far away and picked Ahmed up within thirty minutes. He was excited to learn about the positive identification of Abid as one of the visitors to Frankfurt who Ahmed had escorted, as well as the confirmation of Mahmoud's involvement. To him, it meant that some serious trouble may be brewing in Tampa. In any case, Abe grabbed his cell phone and called George to let him know they were on the way to his office. George alerted Bud Parker. About twenty minutes later, they got to Bud's office. After going through the proper procedures to get their visitor badges, they were escorted to him. His team leaders were there along with a couple of the technical guys.

Bud greeted Ahmed with a smile. Ahmed was a pretty cool guy and doing a great job. The intelligence he'd gathered was tremendously significant. It was becoming more and more critical to bringing the terrorists down at the right moment with each passing day. Not only had he confirmed Mahmoud and Abid's involvement through their travels and use of home and offices, but he had also uncovered the two jihadists, Mohammed and Abdullah. Reported as disappearing from the Frankfort mosque, they had turned up in Tampa. Furthermore, Mohammed had slipped and mentioned that he and Abdullah would be in paradise on Monday. When combined with Abid's reference to two days of hard work because of a schedule change, it became pretty clear to everybody that events were moving much faster to the crisis level than anticipated. Bud had the nagging feeling he was playing catch-up when he should be ahead of the game. As this thought crossed his mind, he asked, "What did you see in the garage, Ahmed?"

"When the garage door went up," he said, "the first thing I saw was a new tan Ford van. It had been backed in with its rear door five feet from a workbench that stretched along the rear wall. Between my two box loads I took a short break and walked to the back of the garage, where I saw that tools were neatly arranged in brackets on the wall. There were radios and TVs sitting on the workbench. Anyone would think it was a repair shop. Of course, I was looking for telltale signs of bomb-making equipment and explosives. It was obvious that the equipment at the workbench was capable of being used, or modified to be used, for bomb preparation purposes, but then that was true of a lot of workshops. The floor was concrete and the van was empty and clean inside and out. There were about ten boxes marked files for different years in the attic. There was nothing that would make one suspicious. My perception is that the garage is important to whatever operation is being planned, but I did not see anything out of the ordinary. As I help Abid tomorrow, my perception may change. I'll just have to wait and see."

"So you are prepared to keep going?" asked Bud.

Ahmed answered quickly, "You bet; I'll call Abid in the morning and tell him I will be glad to help him. Those boxes were very heavy. My suspicion is that they contain weapons and explosives, and I'd like to get a look inside. Who knows, he might trust me a little more and include me in his plans. Even the best of conspirators can get a little careless when pressed with unexpected changes. I believe it is worth a try."

"Okay," said Bud, "it's time to get Department of Justice authorization for physical and electronic surveillance of these guys. Let's go in for an immediate seventy-two-hour request, since the information we have suggests that everything will be over Monday. I'd like to wire Ahmed up in the morning before he goes to help Abid. Maybe we can get Title III permission. It would be great if our tech boys could monitor Abid and Mahmoud's phones over the weekend. Problem is DOJ's reaction on such short notice. I'm doubtful we'll have permission by morning, but it is worth a try. If these guys are going to blow up part of our city, we'd better get every piece of information we can to support their arrests and trials. I do not want them to slip through our fingers because we didn't do things properly or substantiate our suspicions. Ahmed's report leaves no doubt in my mind that we have probable cause, as things are reaching a crisis point demanding our full attention and action.

"Ahmed, check with us in the morning to see if our electronic surveillance request has been approved. If it has, we'll get you wired up; if it hasn't, maybe the tech boys can come up with some other way to let you know when approval has arrived, even though it will be too late to wire you up. I'll leave that to them. They always seem to have some magic they can accomplish. In the meantime, you are an experienced operative. I trust you'll do the right thing regardless of what you encounter."

"I'll do my best. Abid is a leader and thinker, but Mohammed and Abdullah are true jihadist warriors with one-track minds. I don't trust any of them, but Abid's two friends are truly dangerous. My focus will be on them."

With that, Bud gave his team leaders a warning order. He wanted them to stay abreast of this situation, to coordinate with one another, to be prepared to act on short notice, and to make sure the U.S. Attorney was prepared to make himself available should his presence be required to authorize arrests. Things seemed to be developing faster than anticipated.

About that time, George remembered the packet Rick had carried from Atlanta last Friday. He asked one of the agents to get it. It had been sent for fingerprint analysis, and the report had just arrived, showing that Mahmoud and Abid had handled it. Their prints had been available because of the state medical licensing procedures. Now, with everyone watching, he compared the return address to Mahmoud's office street address. What was left of the return address matched his. George gave out a slight sigh that had an "I gotcha" tinge to it because here was positive evidence tying Mahmoud to the Brotherhood. It would help support the surveillance request.

George's cell phone rang. He excused himself and stepped out to take a call from Hannah. She sounded excited and concerned at the same time. It seemed Abid had returned from the noon prayers and gone right into Mahmoud's office. A few minutes later, they were outside with raised voices, arguing with one another. Hannah said she could not understand the entire conversation from her location but it was something about Germany and a changed schedule. Mahmoud didn't think it was necessary but Abid said he didn't call the shots. They parted in a huff but not before Abid made a phone call, with Mahmoud shaking his head. After that, they returned to their offices and patients.

Hannah said because of their conversation yesterday, she thought she should call; nothing like this had ever happened before. George thanked her and returned to Bud's office to inform the group.

Everyone agreed the time schedule for their operation—whatever it had been—was being advanced. This made the situation even more critical. It also signaled the possibility of more errors in their rush to get everything done properly in order to make the new deadline. Obviously, if they were planning an attack, they had to be stopped.

Bud issued more instructions and went back to his office to game-plan the coming events. Looking ahead, he was well aware of the criticality of his agents' actions. If he moved too fast, he might seize the suspected explosives and miss the important people. If he moved too slow, he might miss both the people and the explosives. Loaded vehicles moving around town could be tracked easily enough, but the potential for a tragedy once the jihadists believed capture was imminent made it clear to him that they had to be stopped before they moved. He would try to execute it with the most terrorists at the scene. With that decision made, he settled back to wait for the electronic surveillance authorization.

As Hannah was getting ready to leave her office for the day, one of Abid's friends entered the building and came to her desk. He said he would be cleaning the garage and tuning up the van tomorrow. He needed a key. Since Hannah did not have one, she went to Abid's office and explained the situation. Abid followed her back to the lobby and gave his friend the key. His facial expressions and attitude made it obvious he was aggravated and displeased with his friend. Although no words were exchanged, Hannah got the same message as the visitor.

Mahmoud called Hannah into his office and asked her to work in the morning.

"I'm sorry, but I have made other arrangements and will not be available. However, I asked one of the other girls to stand by in case someone was needed."

Mahmoud wasn't pleased. Nevertheless, he accepted her decision.

"I hope you'll understand," she said.

He smiled with a tired expression. There was no question that he seemed a little edgy today and she couldn't put her finger on the reason.

When she got to the car and was headed home, she called her dad and told him about Abid's friend and Mahmoud's apparent uneasiness. Both incidents made her a little unnerved. She couldn't explain it. Maybe her dad had frightened her a little more than she thought. The atmosphere around the office had changed dramatically in the last twenty-four hours, and she did not like the change.

CHAPTER 21

The Garage and Air Base

Abe drove Ahmed to Bud's office building early Saturday morning. After going through the check-in routine, they were admitted to Bud's office. George was also present. Unfortunately, Bud opened the meeting with, "Our authorization for surveillance has not arrived; that means we can't wire you up this morning, Ahmed. You'll just have to work without it. Maybe it will arrive tomorrow. I'm going to give you a clean cell phone. If you can call any of us during the day, please do. We'll update you, but I doubt we'll be able to wire you up even if permission comes through. You understand there won't be any physical surveillance should you get in trouble. You'll be on your own."

"That's okay, Bud. At this point, I'm really not overly concerned. I think these men will be so busy and focused on what they have to do that not much attention will be paid to me. After all, I was part of the team in Germany, and they really have no reason to question my loyalty. I may not be a jihadist, but to them, I am a loyal Muslim and they know it."

Abe spoke up and said, "I won't be far away in case Ahmed needs help. I have a concealed weapons permit but I don't plan on doing anything unless Ahmed's life seems to be threatened. Additionally, none of these men know me so I can be pretty close without jeopardizing anything."

Bud said, "I am not sure I like what you're saying, Abe."

Abe said, "You aren't doing anything to protect your witness. He's my brother. I will if I have to."

Bud offered, "I guess that is it. I'll be standing by here at the office all day. Plan on coming back here for a debriefing tonight regardless of when you finish up, Ahmed."

With that, Ahmed made his call to Abid, who told him, "Meet me at the garage."

Abe and Ahmed left immediately. Abe dropped him off a short time later and went to a coffee shop down the block. He planned to stick close and move up and down the street during the day.

When Ahmed got to the garage, the door was down. He could see Abid and his two friends moving around, so he walked to the rear side door and entered, saying, "*Sabah el khair*" (Good morning). Everyone reciprocated and Abid shook his hand and said, "It's good to see you. Thanks for coming. Your help will make certain we accomplish our purpose today."

Ahmed responded, "I really appreciate this opportunity. I feel privileged to be helping you and the others and honored that you would let me do so. I am not sure how I can help but I do it for Allah and his glory."

Abid was obviously pleased and said, "It's great having a true believer in our midst. Today, we are going to take some boxes to Mahmoud's garage. Mohammed and Abdullah have been trained in explosives and will be preparing the car in Mahmoud's garage for an operation. Mahmoud is at work so I'd like you to go along and be a look-out while they're working. Tomorrow, we'll be loading the tan van, and I can use you here. We are not expecting any trouble in either place. You know these Americans! They aren't very suspicious or observant, and they play all weekend anyway. Seeing a couple of guys fooling with a car in a garage on a Saturday isn't all that uncommon. Nevertheless, while the men are concentrating on their work, it would not be hard for someone to walk up on them without them being aware of their presence. That could get ugly. We don't want anything like that to happen."

With that, Ahmed joined Mohammed and Abdullah, getting the boxes out of the attic and putting them into the van. When the proper boxes had been loaded, they drove to Mahmoud's home. Mohammed had the garage door opener and promptly opened it. Everything was quiet on the street. They moved quickly to empty the van and bring their supplies into the garage.

Abe had seen them depart and followed at a discreet distance. When he was comfortable with his new observation position, he called Bud and reported their new situation.

Meanwhile, Ahmed watched as the two weapons experts began tearing the car apart and placing the explosives and shrapnel-producing material where it would do the most damage. They took their time and rigged the car with great caution, working right through the lunch hour. They both seemed to be enjoying their work. They joked softly with one another throughout the day. They finished about three and proceeded to load a number of small arms into the car for the two men who had been tasked to take it to its target. By four, they had completed their final checks. With a final prayer to Allah, the three of them left the garage and took the van back.

There hadn't been much conversation during the day. Both Mohammed and Abdullah were very intense while working, but they loosened up as they drove home. Mohammed asked, "Where were you trained, Abdullah?"

He answered, "In Saudi Arabia by Americans and later in Pakistan on the way to fight with Osama in Afghanistan. What about you, Mohammed?"

"I was in the Syrian army and, like you, joined Osama in Afghanistan. In Pakistan, I trained *mujahedeen* for a couple of years, but I wanted to participate in an actual mission. Being selected for an operation in America is the highlight of my life, and I fully intend to make Allah proud of me," answered Mohammed.

Ahmed said, "Both of you know what you're doing. I'd be afraid to do such dangerous work. Will you be part of the attack team with Mahmoud's car?"

"No, both of us will go with Abid. That van will be loaded to the brim and headed for a prime target while Mahmoud's car will make a diversionary attack."

"It sounds complicated but I know your families will be proud of you."

By then they pulled up to the garage and backed the van in, positioning it as previously. It would be easier to load and work on in the morning.

Nobody was around. Ahmed said he'd see them in the morning, called Abe, and met him in front of the office complex. They drove to Bud's office building. It wasn't long before they were in his office with George and the squad leaders.

Having grabbed a cup of coffee on the way in, Ahmed went right into his report. As he finished, a silence fell over the room as Bud considered this new information. Thankfully, everything had gone without incident, but Bud hadn't had a report like this in the entire time he'd been in charge of the Tampa office. The messages between Tampa and Washington were already jamming the airways, and he knew this latest information would stir the pot even more. He broke the silence by saying: "Okay, we know there are two targets and they are in Tampa. We know Monday is the probable day but we don't know the targets or what time they will strike."

Ahmed said, "I know they have powerful explosives. Abdullah mentioned working with C-4 when he trained with the Americans. He commented to Mohammed that it was a really neat explosive because you could mold it any way you wanted to and it would do the job for you. I didn't catch much more of that conversation. I assumed that they were working with it as they prepared Mahmoud's vehicle and that they would also have it for the van. But you couldn't prove it by me, I can't tell one explosive from another. According to Mohammad, Mahmoud's car will be used for the diversionary attack while the van goes after the principal target. Whatever that target might be, the amount of explosives available to blow it up is tremendous, so I would assume major damage, if not elimination of the target. My suspicion is that the diversionary attack will take place first, as it will be a huge distraction for all the first responders regardless of the amount of damage it inflicts."

Bud thought about it for a short time and said, "Based on the information Ahmed has gleaned, his assessment seems logical, but we really need to make every effort to obtain the answers to the questions we don't know." He then announced the FISA request was approved by the DOJ and gave instructions to his tech boys to bug Abid and Mahmoud's office, garage, and residences over the weekend, along with all their communications. He told Ahmed to stop by in the morning to get wired up before heading to Abid's garage. Finally, he directed his counterintelligence unit to execute the surveillance plan for this operation.

Before they broke up, a message arrived from the Detroit office, indicating some increased activity at one of the mosques by suspected Al-Qaeda members. This was enough to put the local Detroit office on a higher alert status and initiate some additional undercover work, but it hadn't gone any further than that. Message traffic indicated Atlanta was quiet although suspicions had been aroused at the field office by the German FBI report.

Meanwhile, Saturday had been a different day for Hannah and the kids. It was their day for a new adventure at the air base with Mark. At breakfast, Thomas was so uptight he was jabbering like an excited chimpanzee and having trouble focusing on eating. Jacqueline ate quietly, without much conversation. Hannah had calmly encouraged both to eat. Outwardly, she played the cool mom, but inwardly she churned with anticipation at the thought of being in Mark's presence. She had no doubt it would be a wonderful day. He would be there soon.

Mark pulled up about 10:30. Johnny was out the door like a rocket. He gave Mark a big hug and ran back in to get everyone moving. The greetings were limited as they climbed in the car. Mark laughed and they were soon happily chatting and joking with one another as they headed to the base. It took about an hour before they arrived at the officers club. After showing them around, they all had a light lunch. Johnny wolfed his food down as if it would be taken away before he could finish. Mark and Hannah tried to slow him down but it was no use. He was convinced he would get to the flight line quicker if his food was gone.

Jacqueline was a perfect lady. There were a number of young officers in the club who were not reluctant to give her the once-over. Every girl knows that a little flirting here and there can lift the spirits and make their day. Learning the game made Jacqueline's day even brighter. Mark knew he and Hannah would have to sit on her a little bit if he became a family member. Like her mother, she was a truly pretty young lady with a certain sophistication belying her years. From Mark's perspective, that could mean trouble, and he made himself a promise it wouldn't happen in his house. He knew Hannah would feel the same way.

Hannah was enjoying the outing. Her family hadn't been on a true adventure like this in years. In fact, they had never experienced anything like this adventure. Mark was the perfect host. It felt so comfortable to be with him. She scared herself sometimes, thinking of Mark as David. They were alike in so many ways. But Mark had a light side to him that everyone admired and wanted to share. He made friends easily and wanted everyone to be at ease. Hannah recognized the power of his personality and the wonderful feeling it gave her to know she was the focus of his attention even when the kids were engaged with him. Liking him was easy. Having him around on a full-time basis would be absolutely wonderful. She was falling in love again and found it absorbing and exciting at the same time. In fact, Hannah felt as young as the first time these feelings had gripped every part of her being years ago.

After lunch, they hit the flight line. Thinking in terms of Jacqueline, Mark had asked one of the young officers if he would escort Johnny and Jacqueline through the KC-135 aerial refueling plane. He said he'd take the cockpit if he'd walk them through the rest of the aircraft. He was waiting as they walked up. Mark took Hannah to the cockpit while Johnny and his sister saw the rest of the plane. He knew it wouldn't take him too long unless the kids asked a lot of questions. Maybe they'd have a chance to be alone for a few minutes. He entered the cockpit, saying, "Come into my office."

She laughed and said, "You are going to explain some of these things to Johnny, aren't you?"

"Oh yes, he'll be sitting right here and I'll go through the whole drill for him."

"He'll love every minute of it, Mark. This is wonderful. I can't thank you enough."

Johnny came into the cabin with Jacqueline and the lieutenant. Mark got out of his seat and told Johnny to take over. He helped Hannah out of the copilot's seat and asked Jacqueline to take her place. He then proceeded to explain a lot of the instruments and talk about flying. When finished, they walked around a couple of jet fighters parked on the runway. Johnny told Mark he'd really like to fly one of those. Mark told him it was fun, he would be able to do so someday if he mastered all his lessons in school.

Heading home, Mark asked if they would like to see a movie.

Hannah said she would prefer to go home and freshen up, have supper, and then go to the movie.

Mark countered, "Okay, what time would you like to have me back to pick you up?"

She said, "No, silly, I meant you are invited to stay for supper and then go to the movie."

"Oh, I thought maybe I was just the transportation …"

"Mark, you are terrible. You knew all along what I meant."

Jacqueline piped up, "Careful, Mom, he's pretty sharp." Everyone laughed.

After the movie, the kids watched a little TV while Hannah and Mark enjoyed a soft drink and some small talk in the kitchen. About ten-thirty, Mark said he'd better get going. Hannah asked him if he had any plans for church. She said they were Presbyterians and asked him to join them for the ten-thirty service in the morning. Mark agreed and asked if he could pick them up. She was delighted with the offer.

He didn't get away without another good-night kiss. This time, Hannah kind of pulled him to her. He responded tenderly, and they stood for a couple minutes, enjoying each other without a care in the world.

CHAPTER 22
Tan Van

Bud's agents really went into action Saturday night and early Sunday morning. By breakfast time, electronic surveillance of all the communications used by the suspects had been fully implemented, and monitoring devices had been planted in frequently used areas. This was accomplished just in the nick of time, as a call was intercepted between Mahmoud and Detroit a little before midnight. After exchanging pleasantries, the person from Detroit said, "We'll see you at 8 AM Monday." With a pleasant good-bye, he hung up. While nothing was definite, most of the agents felt this might be the attack time because it fit with the information Ahmed had obtained as well as the circumstances on the ground in Tampa. Lastly, as the sun came up over Tampa Sunday morning, the physical surveillance plan covering the suspects went into effect.

Ahmed arrived at Bud's office by nine, and the tech boys wasted no time in getting him wired-up. He and Abe were on their way to Abid's by nine-thirty. As he had done the day before, Abe dropped him in front of the office building, and he walked around to the garage.

As Ahmed approached the garage, he saw that his new friends had already begun their work. Several boxes had been placed on the workbench, and Abdullah was struggling with one he'd just brought down from the attic. When he saw Ahmed, he got a big grin on his face and said, "It's your turn."

Ahmed laughed and headed to the attic to retrieve a box while Mohammed said, "You're in for it now."

With that, both he and Abdullah turned to the task of creating a car bomb out of the van, as they discussed the necessity for multiple trigger mechanisms to insure detonation of the bomb in case one failed. Meanwhile, Ahmed dutifully carried the three remaining boxes downstairs. When he finished, Mohammed asked him to open all the boxes. About that time, Abid joined them. Both Ahmed's microphone and recorder as well as the microphone placed in the garage by the tech team were working very well. As a result, Abid could be heard asking Mohammed and Abdullah how things were going. Mohammed answered they had planned well and had everything they needed to do a good job. Abid asked when he thought everything would be ready. The answer he received was that all explosives would be in place about ten that night. With that, he inspected their work and seemed to be well pleased with their efforts. He ordered them to remain on guard duty all night, saying that several people would join them in the early morning, about five-thirty, and that they were bringing their own equipment. Abid told Ahmed to put the weapons under the van seats so they would be easily accessible. As he departed, he said, "I am going to check the other vehicle at Mahmoud's."

Ahmed said, "I'll stay on look-out until Mohammad and Abdullah are finished tonight."

"That's fine, Ahmed. As you heard, they will be on guard tonight, so you won't need to be here. Mohammad will give you some money when you leave this evening. I hope things go well for you in the States. Don't be surprised if some of the brothers contact you in the future. I have told others of your reliability and trustworthiness."

Ahmed couldn't help responding, tongue-in-cheek, "Abid, you are most kind and considerate. May Allah be with you tomorrow and his divine wishes be fulfilled for all of you!"

At that point, Mohammed said, smiling, "Ahmed has been a big help; however, I understand Mahmoud isn't very happy having that vehicle in his garage."

"You're right," smiled Abid. "Mahmoud isn't too keen about Al-Qaeda members conducting this operation. He believes the soft, subtle, disguised, and friendly Muslim Brotherhood approach is preferable, along with having a greater chance for success. We are at odds on this. Pushing the timetable up hasn't helped our relationship any, but orders are orders. This will all be over soon enough." Departing, he added, "Okay, I'll be back about 2:30." Throwing a key at Abdullah, he said, "Meet me at the office. I'll need your help in getting rid of some documents and papers it would be better for the authorities not to find."

Abdullah nodded and continued with his work while Abid drove to Mahmoud's home and inspected the other vehicle. When he departed the garage, he called Mahmoud and told him everything was going to be complete by ten that evening, and he was very pleased with the progress made in such a short time. He said he had a couple of men coming by in the morning, about 5:30, to pick up the car. Mahmoud asked if they would be joining the others, and Abid answered it was better if they went their own way and did their own thing. Mahmoud knew he was right and said nothing. When Abid asked him where he would be in the morning, he said he would be in the office working. Abid agreed this was the best way, considering the future. He said good-bye, adding what a pleasure it had been to have worked with him. Mahmoud reciprocated and they hung up. Abid returned to the office to meet Abdullah.

Earlier in the day, Mark had picked up Hannah and the kids and driven them to church. After the service, he took them all to lunch at the Olive Garden, explaining he loved Italian food. Before leaving the restaurant, Mark inquired as to what everyone was doing that afternoon. Since nobody had any plans, he suggested a walk around the zoo until supper and homework time. They hadn't done this before, and they all agreed it might be fun.

As they were getting ready to leave, Hannah's cell phone rang. It was her co-worker, Jan, who had helped her out at the office while she and the kids visited MacDill AFB. Jan was concerned as to what Mahmoud would find Monday morning. She told Hannah, "There was just too much work for me to accomplish yesterday. My pregnancy didn't help. I got sick and had to depart early. I'm sorry, Hannah, but I wanted you to know there is still a couple hours of work to be accomplished."

Hannah replied, "Don't worry, Jan. I really appreciate your calling. I'll see what I can do. Rest and take care of yourself. I'll see you in the morning."

Turning to Mark and the kids, Hannah explained the situation and said she really needed to go to the office and finish the rest of the paperwork.

Together, her children uttered one great big disappointed moan. At this, Mark offered, "Well, if you two can keep me in tow for a couple of hours, we can let the workaholic go to the office while we go talk to the animals. What do you think?"

With big smiles, they both said simultaneously, "We can! We really can!"

Hannah piped up, "Mark, that isn't necessary."

"I know, but I don't have anything else planned, and I would really enjoy the opportunity of being with these two wild Indians this afternoon."

After a second or two of hesitation, Hannah gave her permission, "Okay, but don't wear Mark out. He's not used to your energy levels."

"Gosh, Mom, I think Mark can handle anything," offered Johnny. "Can't you, Mark?"

"Well, with such confidence, Johnny, I sure am willing to try."

Before they parted, Mark said, "The first one home starts supper." Then with a smile, he added, "We may be a little late." Everyone laughed.

With that, Hannah drove off to the office while Mark and his two charges piled into his Mercedes and headed for the zoo.

Within an hour, the threesome were having a great time observing and talking about the animals.

The kids were very much aware of their mother's interest in Mark and his reciprocal interest in her. Thomas didn't question his mother's relationship with Mark. He was the closest thing to a dad he had ever known, and they were already bonding very well. Jacqueline was not as accepting, although she was well aware of her mother's interest. There was no question that Mark was a nice guy. He had shown sensitivity to her needs as well as her mom's. She enjoyed his willingness to do so as well as his good nature. Even so, the verdict was still out. Mark and Hannah realized Jacqueline was a little more troubled by his courtship, and they were both praying she would be more accepting very soon. All of this made the afternoon more important to both of them.

At the FBI offices, the message traffic intensified all Sunday afternoon. Bud and his team scrambled to stay on top of it. Atlanta remained quiet, with no noticeable change in the level of activity of the suspect currently under surveillance. On the other hand, Detroit had definitely noticed changes in individual routines along with increased activity at one of the mosques.

On the assumption 8 AM was the strike time, Bud wanted everyone in place by 5. His problem remained one of timing because he did not know the targets or their plan of action. The best he could do was estimate that their vehicles would be rolling to their targets thirty to forty minutes before eight. Of course, that theory would go out the window if they had arranged a prestrike assembly area close to the targets. At this point, he knew he had made the right decisions, but there was always a lingering concern he and his team had missed something. Regardless, they were committed to capturing everything and everyone. Surprise was their key weapon, and he prayed that it would be enough.

Bud decided that he and George would be with the strike team at the office garage. George would not advance with the team. He was there as an observer and in case a linguist was needed. Ahmed and Abe were given permission to ride along if they promised to remain in the office building like George. Bud had also made arrangements for a U.S. Attorney to be present when his men went into action. He didn't want any detail to go uncovered. He wanted these men to be captured alive, tried, and convicted for their actions.

Years of experience convinced Bud his team had worked out a good plan. With everything in place, he and George headed home about four to catch a little sleep before their dawn action.

Hannah pulled up to the office about 1:30, let herself in, and went right to work. Her plan was to finish and beat Mark home for supper. It was the least she could do after he'd been so generous with the kids that afternoon. She knew there would be adventure stories, as Thomas could never go anywhere without one or two when he got home. Then, of course, Mark would be there with his own version, while Jacqueline would be the arbitrator, keeping both in line. She smiled as she thought to herself how fortunate and blessed she was to have them all in her life.

Hannah was so deeply engrossed in her work that she did not hear the back door to the office building open. In fact, she didn't notice anything for an hour or two. Then suddenly, she heard a heavy thud coming from Abid's office in the back of the building, followed by some raised voices. She knew that Abid sometimes met with friends in his office, so she wasn't too concerned as she went down the hall to his office. Without hesitation, she opened the door while calling, "Dr. Abid, is that you?"

Before Abid could respond, she was in the room facing both Abid and Abdullah. A filing cabinet had tipped over, and papers were strewn across the floor. Abdullah was in the process of collecting them together. Abid said, "Hannah, what are you doing here?"

"Dr. Mahmoud had some work for me and I couldn't get it done earlier, so I decided to come in today and finish it." As she said this, she was startled to notice two weapons leaning against Abid's desk.

Following her gaze and look of astonishment, Abid knew Abdullah had made a mistake in bringing the weapons into the office. Hannah had seen them and he knew she could not be trusted. If she said one thing to her father, all his planning and hard work would be compromised. That just could not happen. Without any further explanation, Abid told Abdullah to take Hannah to the garage and tie her up in the van.

Hannah blurted, "Why?"

"Because you have blundered into something that is bigger than the both of us, and I cannot let you go until my mission is completed. At this point, you cannot be trusted. I told Mahmoud he shouldn't hire a Lebanese Christian. You know too much about Muslims. So, beautiful

Christian lady, I am afraid your luck has run out. Tomorrow, you will become a statistic of Allah's sword."

"Abid, you do not have to do this. My children need me, and I have been faithful to you and Mahmoud all these years. I don't know what you are planning. Let me go."

"No, you are a filthy Christian, and you will not accept Islam, will you?"

"Never!"

"Then it will give us great pleasure to treat you to hell, and if your children were here, I would help them join you."

Turning to Abdullah, he again said, "Take her to the van while I finish emptying the safe and destroying these papers."

As Abdullah led Hannah to the garage, hidden eyes watched. While it appeared that the woman was being forced along, the surveillance teams weren't absolutely positive she wasn't part of the plot. In any case, Bud and his team leaders were notified of this new development while efforts were undertaken to identify her.

Abdullah wasn't certain he agreed with Abid. Nevertheless, Abid was the leader and he could not disobey his orders. So while he secured Hannah in the van, he told Mohammad and Ahmed what was going on. Neither of them was happy with this development, but they didn't see how it effected their operation in any way so they nodded and went about their business. Of course, Ahmed recognized Hannah from the pictures on George's desk, and he knew he would have to get this information to Bud as soon as he could get away.

Meanwhile, Mark and the kids had a great afternoon and arrived home about four-thirty, expecting to find Hannah busily preparing supper. Disappointed that she was not home, he set about preparing supper as he had promised. To make certain everything would be ready when Hannah arrived, he called her office. Abid answered. When

Mark asked for Hannah, Abid said that she had departed, muttering something about correcting some records or getting some records at Tampa General. He'd been busy and had not paid to close attention to her call down the hall. Anyway, she had a key and could come and go as she pleased.

Mark asked, "Do you have any idea when we might expect her home?"

"No, she left about an hour ago."

"Okay, I'll give her a call on her cell phone. Thanks." With that he hung up and dialed Hannah. Once again there was no response, so he left a message, thinking she might be busy with someone.

When he finished preparing supper, he and the kids sat down to eat. They were famished after their activities at the zoo, and he wasn't particularly concerned about Hannah because she'd said she had a lot to do. On the other hand, she hadn't mentioned running around town and that kind of bothered him, without raising any real concern. It just seemed odd for a Sunday, although in the medical profession, one responded at all times of the day and night.

After supper, he tried both phones again. Nobody answered at the office, and she did not answer her cell phone. It was about six-thirty, and he knew she had not planned to be that late. Mark was now beginning to be a little concerned, but it was time to get the kids working on their homework. He spent a little more than an hour helping Johnny with some math. Jacqueline busied herself with a science project. About eight, he tried again. This time when he got no answer, he asked Jacqueline, "Does your mom ever stop by to check on her parents on the way home?"

"Sometimes, but I don't think she would do that when she knows we are expecting her home."

"I think I'll call anyway," and with that, he dialed George.

George answered, "Hello."

"George, this is Mark Fields. I'm at Hannah's. I took the kids to the zoo this afternoon because Hannah got a call from her co-worker saying she had not been able to get her work accomplished yesterday. Hannah felt she had to go to the office and catch up before tomorrow morning. She was to be back for supper but I have called several times, to no avail. Earlier, Abid told me she had gone to run an errand and he did not know her plans. Has she dropped by your house or contacted you? We expected her home several hours ago."

"No, Mark … you say she went to the office to do some work?"

"That's right, George."

"Let me make a couple of calls and I'll get back to you."

"Okay, I'll be here at the house until I hear from you."

With that, they both hung up, but George immediately called Bud at home. With the current operation under way, he suspected something might have gone terribly wrong. The best-laid plans were often upset by the unexpected, and Hannah's innocent trip to the office might have triggered something sinister. He was very upset as Bud came on the line. He had gotten a call from the surveillance team right after he got home, saying a women had been seen accompanying, or being taken by, one of the jihadists to the garage late this afternoon.

"Bud, this is George. Do you have a description of the woman who entered Mahmoud and Abid's office garage this afternoon? Hannah, my daughter, went to the office to make up some work. She was due home several hours ago and has not returned."

"Yes, George, I was just about to call you. We have finished reviewing the surveillance data and both the video and electronic tapes positively identify Hannah as being held by Abid and one of his friends. She stumbled into Abid's office and was taken to the garage, where Ahmed saw her placed in the van. It looks like Abid plans to make her a part of his show tomorrow."

"Oh, my God! What can we do? I can't let anything happen to her."

"I understand, George. The surveillance boys have done a good job. I was about to let all the teams know your daughter had been identified as the hostage in the garage. Many of our men know her ... this has become personal for them. You know better than most ... they will do everything in their power to save her. Her abduction really doesn't change our plan. It just makes it more dicey for all of us, particularly the assault force."

"I know, but I am scared stiff. Those guys mean business, and if we don't do things exactly right in the morning, we could lose Hannah. Right now, I've got to tell Najwa and then I have to call Hannah's new friend, Mark, who's with the children, and let him know why she isn't home. He's an Air Force colonel at the base, and I don't think he'll want to sit this one out. I sense he's really fallen for Hannah."

"George, I don't mind his accompanying you in the morning, but he has got to stay out of the way. We can't have any cowboy antics. If you think you can handle him, I'll trust him to your care."

"Thanks, Bud. He's a fine young man, and I am certain he can take orders as well as give them. Anyway, he won't have a choice, it is either stay with me and observe, or stay home."

"That's good ... see you at the office. We'll move to the site as planned at five."

With that, they both hung up. George went to find Najwa. His conversation with her was very emotional. When things settled down, he asked, "Would you be willing to go and stay with Thomas and Jacqueline? Mark is at the house now. He's still pretty new to them. I think the kids would be more reassured if you were with them. I am sure they will be upset when they learn of their mother's situation, and while Mark will do anything we ask, I know he would rather be with me in the morning."

Najwa knew he was right and went upstairs to put a few things together.

Then he called Mark and said, "Mark, this is George. We've got a problem …"

CHAPTER 23
Take Down

As George finished telling Mark about Hannah, he suggested Mark might want to spend the night with him and then go with him to Bud's office for the final briefing about four in the morning. Mark accepted his invitation, and after he'd helped Najwa calm the kids and put them to bed, he arrived at George's.

Mark could see that George was very concerned for his daughter. Frankly, Mark was as uptight as he'd ever been, and he'd been in some very tight spots over the years. But this was different. He was falling in love for the first time in his life, and the women he'd selected for his partner had a good chance of leaving this world in the morning. Yes, he was uptight, to say the least. Nevertheless, he made an effort to calm George's fears by commenting, "From what you have explained, it sounds to me as if your FBI friends have done a good job in their planning and preparation for tomorrow. I know there are a number of unanswered questions, but there always will be in such operations. Nonetheless, it seems to me they have done the best they could."

"I know, Mark, I know. I guess I'm just an old guy who believes the odds are in our favor but keeps looking for those unexpected events that will turn a man's hair white in an hour. Hannah's situation qualifies. I'm walking around with my heart in my mouth, functioning on taut nerves, adrenalin, and rage that Abid would make her a part of his game. The thing that gets me the most is that I have known these men for years and never once did I suspect their true colors ... colors that now threaten my own family. In Lebanon, I could have expected something like this after David's death but in the United States ... I let my guard down and I should have been more suspicious."

"George, you just cannot blame yourself. These guys are past masters at deception. If they weren't, none of their tactics would work. I agree that we are often way too trusting. Someday the worm will turn. I hope this happens before it is too late."

Mark changed the subject by saying he needed to call the base and let them know he would not be available for a flight in the morning. George nodded and headed to bed. "I'll wake you at three, Mark."

"Okay, George ... the best thing we can do now is pray ... I'm not sure I'll be able to sleep."

Both agreed it would be hard to get the "what-ifs" out of their minds. There was so much at stake.

The alarm really didn't wake George, it just told him it was time to get moving. When he went to get Mark, he found him sitting on the bed and remarked, "Boy, we sure are a couple steel-nerved guys." They both laughed and proceeded to dress. They grabbed a donut and cup of coffee as they headed out the door. George drove as Mark wasn't that familiar with the location of his office complex.

After the final briefing, everyone headed to their respective positions, and by five Monday morning, both of the jihadist sites had been surrounded. All Bud needed to do was give the signal. The goal was to capture as many of the jihadists as he could without bloodshed on either side. Not knowing their strike plans, he wasn't sure what to expect. Several unanswered key questions bothered him. Would both vehicles head for their objectives at the same time, or go at different times? Would the men joining Abid be suicide bombers or just fighters? Would they have already armed themselves or would that be done as they assembled in the garages? Should he attack before or after they got in the vehicles? When he attacked and they saw they could not win, would they detonate the explosives or surrender? Did they have communications with the other group? Ahmed had reported Abid planned to take Hannah with them, but would he?

Suddenly, the team leader at Mahmoud's house was on the radio talking to him. He had only seen one additional person join the guard in the garage that morning but the garage door had begun to open and he thought they were getting ready to move the car to a pre-attack position or the target. He wanted to know if he should try to seize them now. Bud didn't think he had a choice, and he gave the attack order and sat back to wait. It was about a quarter to seven.

As the assault commenced, he monitored the team's communications. He could hear everything. At the last minute, they had been spotted and a few shots were exchanged. Thankfully, surprise had carried the day. There were no casualties. The car and all the jihadists' equipment had been seized. It did not appear they had time to warn Abid's group in the other garage. Bud breathed a sigh of relief and turned his attention back to his own immediate problem.

Bud knew that Abid's group would be moving soon. He did not know where they were going but it was seven o'clock. If he and his team had interpreted the intercept correctly, it wouldn't be long now because of the traffic and distance to their target. He ordered his assault team to get as close to the garage as possible.

When the team got within fifteen to twenty feet of the front and back doors, the big garage door began to open. There was no more waiting. Orders were shouted. The assault team advanced at a run and was in the garage before the jihadists knew what hit them. Nevertheless, one of the more alert and quick-reacting jihadists fired several shots. He was gunned down immediately but not before he had wounded two men. Getting the jihadists away from their equipment, searched, and out of the assault area took first priority for the team. Simultaneously, the medical personnel Bud had ensured were present tended to the two wounded.

George, Mark, and Abe had been faithful to Bud's instructions and had not advanced to the garage until the assault was over and the captured men were seized. Ahmed had remained behind. He didn't want to be recognized. He knew he might be needed at a future trial to explain his taped conversations but hoped the surveillance evidence would be sufficient for a guilty plea. Ahmed liked being in the shadows because he was most effective operating there. He wanted to get out of the business, but on his own terms. To him, that meant he and the people he worked for were the only ones having knowledge of his business and identity. That was always the better way, and he felt no need to change it at this time.

Bud was the first in their group to get to the back of the van. George and Mark were a step behind. As they got to the door, a couple of his agents were in the process of untying Hannah and removing her from the van. When she saw them, she let out a cry of joy. The relief on all their faces told the whole story. Bud and George reached out and gave her a quick hug but she fell into Mark's arms, sobbing with happiness. Neither of them said anything. At that moment, holding tightly to one another was simply enough. Words would come later. As their embrace ended, they walked slowly out of the garage to the ambulance. George followed closely behind, saying nothing. He knew these were special moments in their lives, and he did not want to break the magic. As the medics were finishing, Bud walked over to check on her. Mark said, "She will be fine, Bud. You and your men did an outstanding job this morning. Thanks for allowing me to be around. I owe you one. When Hannah has recovered, we'll have to get together."

"Yes," Hannah said, "that would be wonderful."

"I'll look forward to it," replied Bud. "In the meantime, I hope you can put this behind you quickly, Hannah."

"I'll try ... I have some new incentives to do so ... right now, I need to get home to the kids."

"Okay, see you soon." With that, George and Mark led her to the car and they headed home.

It was over. The relief was complete. The adrenalin was subsiding. The sense of accomplishment was exhilarating. Yet for all of the team, the magnitude of the jihadists' attempt, the fact it was in their hometown, and the realization as to how close it had come to being successful stunned everyone. And the knowledge there would be other attempts was frightfully depressing.

By the time everyone had returned to the office, Detroit had reported seizing a portion of the jihadist team before they could initiate their operation. However, the other section had made a run for it. A high-speed chase had followed, with the jihadist vehicle leaving the roadway, striking a tree, and exploding. Fortunately, traffic was light in the area at the time. Only two cars and a trailing police car were blown off the road by the force of the explosion. One civilian was killed and all the others were in the hospital with serious injuries. While not a total success, Mike Phillips, the Agent in Charge, hoped interrogation would reveal the entire plan.

Washington was complimentary in both cases. But their focus was on the information to be gleaned from the interrogations, the situation in Atlanta in particular. In Tampa, Bud had asked all of those arrested if they wanted lawyers. Both Mahmoud and Abid said they weren't necessary right now. From their perspective, they were warriors in Allah's army and he would protect them by providing them with the knowledge they needed to thwart the kafir interrogators if they wanted to do so. They knew nothing bad was going to happen to them while in custody. Americans were soft-bellied snakes who were afraid of their own power and failed to use it even in the face of proven enemies who had killed mercilessly. Who would be afraid of such adversaries? Their haughty attitudes, repeated propaganda lines, and disdain for their captors made their conversations interesting, explosive, but tedious.

While his agents did the interrogation, Bud had George chomping at the bit to take a crack at Mahmoud, but Bud's superiors didn't care for the idea. They knew he was a naturalized citizen who'd worked with them for years and held a Top Secret clearance, but they wanted him held in reserve until things had settled down a bit. That didn't make sense to Bud, because he believed Mahmoud held some critical information needed right now. In fact, Bud actually thought George was the ideal person to deal with Mahmoud since he was a Beirut University graduate and fellow alumni member. Further, having worked with the forerunners of Hamas and Hezbollah years earlier, they might have the best chance of directing any willingness to talk in such a way as to get the most accurate information the quickest. One thing was certain, Hamas was the militant arm of the Brotherhood started in Palestine, and there was a lot of connectivity of its members with those in the United States.

It didn't take long to determine that Mahmoud wasn't a fighter. His verbal battles with the interrogators led to some explosive moments, but they quickly realized that he was a bag of wind. He opened up quickly once a little verbal pressure was applied concerning his forthcoming lifestyle. Then, too, Mahmoud thought that providing some information would give him a greater opportunity for clemency, even though the FBI agent had told him he could not offer any deals. Of course, there was his dislike of Abid and Al-Qaeda's open policy of killing innocent civilians, Muslim and non-Muslim. Mahmoud was an intellectual who believed in Allah's message but confined his fighting techniques to the subtle, deceptive, and under-the-table activities of the Brotherhood. He knew of its militant adventures and the connectivity between various Muslim organizations in the States but believed himself a more effective warrior as a friendly clandestine fifth column operative.

Mahmoud told them the plan had been to have a diversionary attack with the car in his garage in downtown Tampa. He said Abid had talked about setting off the bomb in front of the exploding chicken sculpture next to the Sykes Building at Kennedy and Ashley during the morning rush hour. He'd laughed about the picture of that sculpture disintegrating as panic and traffic entanglements stopped everything downtown during the morning. He believed civilian casualties would be significant at the intersection as well as from flying glass in the surrounding buildings. At the last minute, he changed his diversionary target to the Federal Building. An explosion there would make it seem more intentional. If they blew up the exploding chicken, some might think it was an accident and consider them inept, and he did not want that to be anyone's impression.

The prime target was to be either the departure or arrival areas at the airport. It was thought the amount of explosives used could damage both areas. Economically, it could have a heavy impact for several months. Osama had adamantly talked about destroying the American economy. Of course, after 9/11 Mahmoud had been surprised at the amount of fear permeating the United States, as most people thought they would be the next target. He laughed at this and said such attacks really work from the perspective of raising the fear level.

The part of Mahmoud's story occupying everyone's immediate attention dealt with the fact Atlanta had not been able to advance their attack along with Tampa and Detroit when the order had come to do so. Mahmoud had no idea when the cell in Atlanta would act, although he expected it to be the following week. As in Tampa, jihadists had arrived or would soon be arriving from other countries to participate. Mahmoud had no idea what their targets were, but suspected they would be similar to the selections made in the other two cities.

When Bud heard this news, all message traffic stopped in order to get this information to headquarters. He called a meeting at his office in an hour. He specifically asked for George, Ahmed, and Abe.

Immediately following the initial interrogations, Mahmoud and Abid were given preliminary hearings before the U.S. Magistrate. Although they did not want legal representation, the magistrate appointed an attorney for both men. This case was just too important and he didn't want to take any chances that some small misstep might negate the success of the FBI's operation. When they were unable to make their bonds, both were remanded to the custody of the U.S. Marshalls and taken to jail.

George had dropped Mark and Hannah off, picked up Najwa, and taken her home before getting involved observing the interrogations.

By lunchtime, things had pretty much returned to normal at Hannah's. The kids had stayed home from school all morning, but Hannah felt the best thing for them would be school in the afternoon. They protested a bit, but they lost. Mark took them to school and returned to the house. He hadn't been alone with Hannah since the incident, and he sensed they needed to talk.

When he returned, he found Hannah in the kitchen having just brewed a steaming pot of coffee along with some cookies she and Jacqueline had baked that morning to keep busy. The scene was very peaceful and the aroma tantalizing. As he entered, he couldn't help but smile and say, "Wow! What a wonderful setting to come home to. Twenty hours ago, I wasn't certain this would be possible."

"Mark, it took every bit of my strength not to cry through the whole ordeal. I was frightened out of my wits. I know what jihadists can do. I've seen it with my very eyes. Their brutality and barbarism is unfathomable. Even though you have read all the terrible things in the Koran, Hadith, and Sira, the horror of their actions is incomprehensible. When Abid told me I would accompany them in the van to the target, I had no doubt that I would be blown up in the morning along with their target. Millions of things went through my mind ... particularly what was going to happen to the kids. Because of them, my anxiety level hovered at the highest level it could without destroying me right then. To have lost their father and then ... then ... possibly me too ... it was horrid to think about, and I anguished about it all night. Simultaneously, as a Christian I kept praying for strength and courage and God's will, knowing that he would be with me and see me through. At these times, I experienced that joy and peace only he can provide in such circumstances. Nevertheless, being a fickle human being, my captivity was a nightmare as I vacillated between these two thoughts. It was terrible."

"I know, Hannah," responded Mark. "I was going through something similar ... didn't sleep all night. All I wanted to do was get in on the fight to save you. Over the course of the last few days, you have become the focus of my life, and I would do anything not to see that change. In fact, these last few hours have made me realize that I love you more than anyone I have ever loved, and I want you to be my wife. Your kids are extraordinary. The kids and I seem to get along well. I want their permission to join your family. At the same time, I want you to know I will suffer greatly as we await their decision because I want you now. You are too precious to me … the last twenty-four hours have demonstrated that very clearly. Will you be my wife?"

"Oh, Mark, my heart tells me the same thing, and my answer is yes! However, we must give the kids a chance to adjust to this idea. I think your idea about getting their permission has merit but I don't know what we'll do if they don't give it."

"Honey, under the circumstances, I believe the Lord is in this all the way. We may have some ups and downs but I don't believe he would keep me single all these years and allow me to fall in love with you and your family without some pretty extra special advance planning. Believe me … based on my life, he is here. I am convinced he has brought us together so that we might be one. My heart tells me you sense this also. With him at the center of our marriage, how can we fail? I just do not believe that is possible." With that said, Mark slowly put his arms around her, held her tight, and kissed her. They both realized they had set a new course and were almost giddy at the prospects for the future. While this exchange was transpiring, their coffee got cold. In their moment of truth, they had completely forgotten anything else. Yes, love was definitely in bloom.

As reality broke through the clouds of euphoria, Hannah realized Mahmoud and Abid's patients would be anxious to know what was going on. She called her dad and asked if she should go to the office and start notifying everyone that the office was closing. George told her not to worry about the patient list. Some of the administrative staff would get them notified. He went on to say, "I'm up to my ears right now. You keep Mark under tow today. He'll have to go back to work tomorrow. I'll check to see if your help could be useful in sorting through some of the doctors' office papers. If so, they can contact you tomorrow. At this moment, everything is pretty much a frenzy here."

"Okay, Dad. The kids will be coming through the door shortly. I love you."

"Love you too, honey."

George and the FBI team were indeed busy. Following the arrest, the U.S. Attorney scheduled a news conference for Tuesday morning at 10:00 AM, and they needed to assist in the preparation of the release. Based on past experiences, they knew that Mahmoud and Abid would be screaming for journalists to hear their stories. Nothing their lawyers could tell them would hold them back. They would do everything to damage the prosecution. By talking to the press as soon as possible, they believed they could create sympathy for themselves and their cause. Maybe they could effectively rebut and perhaps misdirect the focus of the evidence against them before it was officially released. By denying connectivity to other groups and Al-Qaeda, it was possible to provide the basis for propaganda initiatives by friendly organizations and nations in support of their clemency and cause.

Working together, the U.S. Attorney's Office and Bud had collaborated to get the statement together, and at 10:00 AM Tuesday morning, it was briefed to the local and national news organizations. All involved received laudatory comments but no names were released. The critical point was that a terrorist group had been located in Tampa and was stopped before they did damage, while a similar operation in Detroit had not been so successful. The reality made everyone take notice for the moment, but many simply went back to their routines with apathy in their hearts. While they didn't like it, those who put their lives on the line every day were painfully aware of society's shortcomings when it came to the truth about fighting jihadists. And so, such incidents would happen again. Everyone prayed law enforcement would meet the challenge before a catastrophe happened.

CHAPTER 24
Ahmed in Atlanta

Mahmoud's information on Atlanta created a lot of concern. Bud had called a special meeting at which he asked the attendees what the office might do to assist in capturing the jihadists before they struck. George said he didn't have to think about that too long. If Ahmed was game, he needed to be sent to Atlanta to help identify any of the jihadists, just as he had done in Tampa. There wasn't any question this would be a good idea.

While Ahmed agreed this was a good idea, he was reluctant to keep playing the role of a Muslim. After some more discussion, he said he would go if they would promise not to call on him again. Bud said he would personally see what he could do. In the meantime, he was going to contact the Agent in Charge of the Atlanta office and tell him of Ahmed's willingness to help. Before he made the call, George reminded Bud his son, Thomas, spoke Arabic and would make a good escort for Ahmed if it could be arranged.

About an hour later, a message arrived thanking Ahmed for his willingness to help and telling him Thomas would be his contact. After all the flight arrangements had been made, George called his son and filled him in on recent events and the criticality of Ahmed's assistance in Tampa. He also gave him Ahmed's flight information and asked to meet him tomorrow morning.

The flight and pick-up was uneventful. Ahmed couldn't get over how much Thomas looked like his dad and commented they looked as if they'd been cloned. Thomas laughed and acknowledged the similarity. In fact, he said he'd been mistaken for his dad at one of the FBI conferences he'd attended. The person who made the mistake was a little embarrassed when she saw them together a few minutes later. He said he and his dad had had a lot of fun with this over the years.

Ahmed had asked about the various mosques in town and had been told there were several with questionable attendees. Thomas selected the one most likely to have troublemakers, taking Ahmed there first. It was just before noon when he dropped him off. They agreed to meet down the street in about an hour or hour and a half.

As in Tampa, Ahmed tried to stay inconspicuous. The mosque was larger and more open. Even so, he positioned himself where he could observe without being detected. Just before the service started, he noticed two men enter; he had seen them in Germany at one of the retreats. In fact, he remembered one of them as having gone to Afghanistan for several months. This time, Ahmed decided not to take the chance of being identified. He rose and slowly moved out of the hall. He went directly to the meeting place and told Thomas what he had seen. They decided to follow the men when they exited the mosque.

Thirty minutes later, they observed the men headed for their car and tailed them to an apartment complex. That had been so simple but it was the years of undercover work that was really paying off. Thomas was struck by the dedication of men like Ahmed. He hoped he could always be as faithful to his country.

As they were driving back to the office, Thomas said he and his wife Alice were having supper with a lady from southern Lebanon that evening. She worked with freshman foreign students at Georgia Tech, helping them assimilate. He was certain Ahmed understood a lot of the problems these kids faced when they hit our culture. He went on to say she was about Ahmed's age, and it would be nice if he joined them. Since he didn't have anything else to do that evening, he accepted Thomas's invitation.

The restaurant was downtown, and Thomas had asked Ahmed to be there at six-thirty. Being new to Atlanta, he didn't realize the traffic problems and arrived late. As he was escorted to the table, he saw Thomas and Alice facing him. Their supper partner had her back to him. When Ahmed got to the table, he looked down at his dinner partner, with incredulity written all over his face, and stopped in his tracks. It was Maria, his one and only love.

Maria stood and they embraced. They both were overcome with emotions. Tears of happiness and excitement flowed freely down their cheeks as Thomas and Alice looked on in questioning amazement. It took several minutes before either spoke intelligently. Finally, Ahmed turned to his hosts and slowly told them the story of their love and separation. By the time he finished, Alice was in tears and Thomas had a lump in his throat.

When Ahmed stopped talking, Maria told of her life since they had last seen one another, and then Ahmed did the same thing. He had remained a bachelor. Maria had married, had two children, lost her husband, and came to America with her family. Contact between them had been lost a long time ago. It was apparent this was not important as they proceeded to pick up where they left off. In fact, it was fascinating to watch the love they had for each other being rekindled before their eyes.

All of this getting reacquainted dominated the table conversation for the rest of the evening. Thomas and Maria never did get to discuss the intended purpose of their supper meeting. Maria had some concerns about possible members of Hamas and Hezbollah in her student group. She wanted to alert Thomas and get some advice. It did not happen, and as they were leaving, they agreed to meet again in a few days. Ahmed offered to take Maria home. She accepted and agreed to have supper with him the next evening.

Ahmed was happier than he'd been in years. He felt like a young boy again. Best of all, he sensed Maria was having a similar experience, and this meant his life might possibly change in a big way in the not-too-distant future. Thomas did not have to be a mind reader to understand what was happening. And he really wasn't surprised when Ahmed told him he was staying over and would see Maria again that evening. The next question came as a little bit of a surprise. Ahmed asked if there might be a job for him as a translator or something in the Atlanta office. Thomas said he'd look into it but it may take a little time. Ahmed said that was fine because he was thinking of moving to Atlanta. Thomas winked and said he just couldn't understand this sudden change in him. They both laughed.

That evening, Ahmed and Maria barely touched their food as they talked of the past and the future. They had a wonderful time together. Ahmed told her he had made up his mind to move to Atlanta, that he had never stopped loving her, he wanted to court her again, and if things worked out, he wanted to fulfill his youthful dream of marrying her. Maria felt the same way; it had been a long time ago, and she believed they needed some time to get reacquainted before any major decisions were made. Even so, he asked, "Can we be engaged? I have always thought of you as my love and having a ring on your finger would mean a lot to me." She agreed and they embraced with a renewed commitment in their hearts.

At the same time, Maria updated Ahmed about her two sons: Paul, twenty-four, and John, twenty-two. She knew being engaged would cause them some concern. Paul had married out of college at Northwestern and was in the computer information business. He and his wife, Amy, lived in Chicago and had presented Maria with her first grandchild, Lauren, a year ago. John was doing some graduate work at Moody Bible College and was also in Chicago. He'd met a young lady but his studies dominated his thoughts at this point. He had evidenced some interest in Middle East missionary work. He had a good command of Arabic. Maria wasn't too happy about this but she knew her son would listen to the Lord. She would have to be happy with his direction in his life. One thing was certain. The boys were very close to and protective of their mother. They wanted her to be happy, but she knew they would scrutinize every aspect of Ahmed's character with a fine-tooth comb. Time would be needed to satisfy all their questions and concerns. Nevertheless, Maria knew Ahmed would pass all their tests. It was only a matter of time.

Back in Tampa, Hannah was experiencing a hard time. No matter how she tried, the terror of that night in the van haunted her. She had been so close to death, without any hope of being saved. Her sudden and unanticipated rescue had left her thrilled but grasping for a sense completion. She kept having sensations of being in the van without the rescue. Everybody understood and offered the compassion she needed to help her heal. Even so, it would take time. Mark and the kids were particularly solicitous. And as they worked together to help Hannah free herself from her anxiety, they bonded in ways that made family a reality in their lives instead of a future possibility. Within a short time, the kids came to recognize Mark as a stepfather. They witnessed the love he had for their mother in a thousand ways each day. As they watched, their hearts could not help but accept him as a new member of their family. George and Najwa were thrilled as well as all their friends.

George had thought it important to tell Hannah everything about the two doctors. Bud agreed. When the newspapers discovered she'd been a hostage, they would be clamoring for a story. It was better that he review things with her now than later.

Like her father, Hannah was still having a little trouble believing the worst of Mahmoud and Abid, even though the evidence was overwhelming at this point. However, as the truth crystallized in her mind, she talked it out with Mark. He was a fantastic listener and had comforted her with words and reassuring arms as the horrid tale of what Mahmoud and Abid had planned unfolded. He knew the truth would make all the difference to her recovery. Regardless, having been deceived the way she had for so many years was devastating. She just could not get over the fact she'd worked side-by-side with those men without the slightest hint of their deadly clandestine plans. That was almost as frightening as being held prisoner. It was also a point the press would use to raise nasty questions in their interviews. After all, how could one who worked so closely with someone not know their plans? Of course, for Hannah, the more pressing problem now was, which of her friends could she trust? At this point, that was a devastating and almost debilitating thought.

Being without a job also heightened her tension. Of course, Mark didn't miss the opportunity to reassure her that he knew where there was a job for life if she'd have him. Hannah was delighted with his idea. Most importantly, she saw the kids and Mark bonding much quicker than either of them had anticipated. She was overjoyed. Sometimes, she had to pinch herself. As the nightmare faded, she praised God for his goodness. He was truly making all things new in her life.

In an effort to help her get active again, Mark also made some inquiries at the base about the possibility of a job. They were always looking for good help because of the turnover, and he was hoping something would come together soon.

On balance, considering everything that had happened, Hannah was struggling but on the mend. Mark's fears of losing her were being replaced with a deeper sense of commitment and love. This horrible event was making them stronger, making them all stronger. Indeed, the future held much promise, and they both knew it.

CHAPTER 25

Disappointment

On Wednesday afternoon, Rick called Sam. He was a little down in the dumps. Ed Townsend had gone ahead and published his political Islam article and came under a lot of fire, particularly from Muslim groups. It is true his article brought more calls, E-mails, and letters than any other article in years, but Ed had a thin skin and wasn't about to create waves. When different Muslim groups began to call his paper racist, Islamaphobic, anti-Muslim, hate-filled, and a target for jihadists, the intimidation worked; he told Rick he would not assist him in publishing any additional articles on Islam that were not politically correct.

"It is so interesting to me that people will not check out the truth before taking a side," Rick said to Sam. "If he had, he would have found my article was 100 percent factual, historically accurate, and contained information of great importance to all of us. Like so many, he did not do that even though I told him there was no substance to the unsubstantiated claims of those who called. Regardless, the threat of lawsuits drove the nail home and he closed me out. I suppose that is happening to others around the country when they challenge the claims of political Islam, or any part of it. What a shame! I tried to hold my cool using freedom of speech and the truth as my rationale for continuing, but he would have none of it. In the end, we exchanged some harsh words, with my calling him a collaborator and his calling me an ungrateful bastard. I don't think we are irreconcilable but it will take a long time.

"Sam, from what I hear, the Muslim Brotherhood and Al-Qaeda have been pretty active in Tampa these last few days. I would really like to do a story on the Brotherhood especially since I met Mahmoud at the alumni party. I thought I might try to interview him while he is in custody."

"Well, I don't know, Rick, I am pretty sure you won't get anything more than his propaganda line. These guys all seem to be pretty good at deflecting the truth about their activities. Nevertheless, I'd give it a try. Maybe his lawyer would permit him to do an interview with you. I am sure George can get the attorney's phone number for you."

"That would be great, Sam. Oh, before I forget, our plane arrives the same time as last week. I'll buy supper if you'd like to stop on our way home. Ask Trudy and see what she says. We are game for anything."

"Okay, Rick, I'll try to call back this evening."

About nine that night, Sam phoned to say he'd gotten the lawyer's number and called him on Rick's behalf. The lawyer had agreed to speak to Mahmoud and see if he would be willing to talk to him. Sam said, "Mahmoud has been a little preoccupied with the FBI this past week, but toward the weekend, you may have an opportunity to get together for a brief time at the jail.

"That's okay, I'll see him any time he wishes."

"That's fine, Rick, but you do understand that you are setting yourself up to be a trial witness by interviewing Mahmoud, don't you?"

"I hadn't thought about that, Sam, but this story seems worth the chance," replied Rick.

"It may be, Rick, but I just thought a reminder was in order. Perhaps something can be set up for Friday afternoon. With the arraignment being over and his future in little doubt, I'll bet he'll want to talk to you or any other journalist he can entice to hear his story so it can be published to the world."

"That's great. I'm sure Ann and I will be tired of looking at houses by then. If not, Ann can continue while I break off. Thanks, Sam. I'll call his attorney and see if a Friday meeting can be arranged. See you Thursday evening. Love to Trudy ..."

CHAPTER 26

Return to Tampa

Their last evening in Atlanta, Ahmed and Maria talked late into the night. Ahmed was beside himself; now that he had found her again, he wanted to be with her. He had asked if she would accompany him back to Tampa. At first she was reluctant, but Ahmed eventually prevailed. He called Abe and asked him if it would be all right to bring Maria as a houseguest. Abe didn't hesitate. He knew how important Maria was to Ahmed. It would be a wonderful opportunity for all of them to get reacquainted, and it would give Cynthia the chance to get to know her. They had plenty of room at the house.

Abe and Cynthia were at the airport to greet them. Their happy expressions as the two of them came through the gate arm-in-arm told the whole story. The years may have brought some physical change but their hearts were as young as they ever had been.

As they drove home, Ahmed announced their engagement. He followed this news with the caveat that Maria said they needed a courtship period because so many years had passed. She'd also let him know he must become a Christian in the presence of his family and friends. She would not accept any more of his role-playing as a silent

Christian and public Muslim. That had to come to an end immediately. He didn't even have to think twice about his answer.

Ahmed told Abe he would like to make his confession of faith Sunday morning if possible and asked Abe what church he was attending. Cynthia said they went to the United Methodist Church in Brandon. Abe would call the pastor when they got home to see if he would do the honors.

The conversation bubbled forth in a lively manner all the way home. Ahmed announced he would be moving to Atlanta so his courtship of Maria would not be interrupted in any way. He wanted to be with her every day. They had a lot to learn about one another before tying the knot, and he wanted to be in the right place to insure it happened quickly. In almost the same breath, he told Abe that George's son, Thomas, was a great young man and had been a big help to him while in Atlanta. Before returning to Tampa, Thomas had told him once he became a citizen he'd be willing to put in a good word for him anytime he applied for a job, perhaps even as a translator for the FBI in Atlanta. Obviously, that would be perfect.

Abe and Cynthia hardly got a word into the conversation. Abe was thrilled at this turn of events because he knew of his brother's deep love and commitment to Maria. He had never dreamed they would see one another again. He avoided conversations about things of the heart with Ahmed because he knew how his had been broken. To Abe, this whole turn of events was an absolute miracle. He'd experienced the Lord's work before and was convinced he was right in the middle of another one right now. Abe was so happy for his brother, he hardly knew what to say. He just kept praising the Lord for his graciousness.

In the afternoon, Rick and Ann arrived on schedule and were met by Sam and Trudy. True to Rick's suggestion, Sam headed back to the Colonnade for supper, saying he could not turn down a free meal under any set of circumstances. Their conversation was light and highlighted by Rick's news of his recall to active duty with assignment in Tampa. The girls never stopped talking about housing areas, public and private schools, malls and shopping, cultural activities, and the anticipation of all those things that make a move exciting. Exciting until the actual day comes with its good-byes, boxes, the moving van and personnel, the house selling and buying on the other end, along with the myriad paperwork, phone calls, and resultant exhaustion. Oh yes, all these things and so much more.

Rick told Sam that his conversation with Mahmoud's attorney had gone well. In fact, Sam's assessment of Mahmoud's desires was 100 percent accurate. He wanted to talk and Rick would be one of the first journalists to speak with him. Although Rick wasn't certain he'd learn much, one never knew what insights would be gained. It was just a wonderful opportunity to actually be able to talk to a clandestine member of the Brotherhood, and Rick prepared for their conversation as best he could with the limited published information. He knew the history but not much about the extent, depth, and effectiveness of their operations.

After explaining all this to Sam, Sam told him George would bring him up to date on the happenings in Tampa that were available for public consumption before the interview so he'd be on top of things as he sat down with Mahmoud. Rick said he couldn't ask for a better situation. He'd really considered himself extremely fortunate his first visit to Tampa in meeting all of Sam's Beirut University friends. There was no way he could have planned his part in these developments any better. Sometimes, you just had to sit back and go with the flow, so to speak, and this was one of those times. He was very grateful.

Just then the phone rang. It was Mahmoud's attorney. He simply said Mahmoud wanted to see him at 2 PM tomorrow.

Rick answered, "That's great, I'll be there. Thanks!"

Turning to Ann and his hosts, he said simply, "We are getting together at two tomorrow."

As the evening came to a close, Ann thought it would be better if they started house hunting in Carrollwood in the morning, then Brandon and northwest Tampa on Saturday if they hadn't found something by then. This schedule would also have the best chance of putting Rick in close proximity to the location for his appointment. Tomorrow was going to be a big day.

Before they headed to bed, Rick called Mark to check on him and see if anything had developed with Hannah. Ann was beside herself with questions. He told Rick what had been going on and said they would be at Sam and Trudy's tomorrow evening for supper. Rick told Mark he was happy things seemed to be working out for them and Ann would probably be cornering him to get all the details. He left him with the warning, "You'd better be ready." They both laughed as they hung up.

CHAPTER 27

Interview

Rick and Ann were up with Sam and Trudy bright and early Friday. It was a beautiful, clear morning. Their forty-minute walk gave everyone a good appetite, and Trudy pulled her normal magic with breakfast. During their discussions, Ann asked if Trudy would like to go house hunting with them. Because of Rick's appointment, she figured having Ann with her would give her company and someone to share ideas with as she investigated the different homes she visited. Trudy thought it a great idea, as she knew the Realtor Ann would be working with over the weekend. Once that was settled, they all headed for Carrollwood and some homes the Realtor thought would be appropriate based on the information Ann provided earlier. After visiting several over a three-hour period, they had lunch at Perkins and took Rick to George's office.

George sat down with Rick as planned. He couldn't tell him much more than what the FBI had released about the planned jihadist operation earlier in the week. But it did give them both a chance to review some of Mahmoud's history as well as the history and media information about the Brotherhood before talking to him. Rick was grateful for any opportunity to talk with someone as knowledgeable as George. Both he and George attributed the capture of the jihadists to Ahmed and Abe. They were the catalysts around which the operation had come to fruition. While nothing would ever be published publicly, both men undoubtedly would be recognized for their activities by the FBI and, perhaps, even the president. Rick said he hoped this would happen as they were very deserving from his perspective.

Bud Parker came in just about that time to thank Rick for bringing the Muslim Brotherhood document to them. It had proved to be another important clue in the chain of events leading to the surveillance and capture of the jihadists. Rick was appreciative of his remarks and thanked him. With that, Bud excused himself, and George took Rick to see Mahmoud where he was being held in custody by the U.S. Marshalls.

As he entered the room where Mahmoud had been taken for the interview, Rick greeted Mahmoud and reminded him of the Beirut University function where they had met. He remembered and told Rick it was nice to see him again, although he wished it could have been under better circumstances. Rick agreed with him and explained he would like to do a story about him, his team members, his involvement with the jihadists, and the Muslim Brotherhood.

Mahmoud smiled and offered that he probably wouldn't uncover any information that hadn't already been published.

Rick countered that more and more information was becoming available each day because of the many operations the Brotherhood was conducting, which were gradually being compromised. He went on to say he had never knowingly met a member of the Brotherhood, and he was having trouble fitting Mahmoud into the mold of a clandestine operative he had envisioned when thinking about this group.

Mahmoud chuckled and said that was interesting because it verified the significance of individuals like him being involved in this battle. He said his day-to-day life as a friendly doctor automatically lessened the likelihood he could or would be living a secret life and that was the beauty of the Brotherhood.

Rick concurred in the effectiveness of the disguise and said he had read the works of Hassan el-Banna and Sayyid Qutb and understood their desire to get back to Islam's fundamentals, although he had a great deal of trouble with the killing of innocents. He went on to say this seemed to be contrary to the Hippocratic oath Mahmoud lived by as a doctor and thus made it difficult for him to understand why Mahmoud would be involved.

Mahmoud said, "The simple answer to your question is that Allah directs my life. You Americans do not have the faith you had in previous years. The secular nature of your government and society is offensive to Allah and all Muslims. I would wager that is true within your own culture but you have allowed the few to dictate to the majority and developed an apathetic approach to all those who are encroaching on your freedoms in the name of the very freedoms you flaunt to the rest of the world. And it is your freedoms that are being used against you in every way imaginable."

"Okay, I can agree we have a soft belly, but I do not see any of this as being an excuse to kill innocents."

"No, but Allah does and he is very specific about using all methods of warfare to make Islam the religion of the world."

"Mahmoud, in my religion, Jesus came and died for my sins. That makes a lot more sense to me than killing in the name of Allah and dying to get to heaven."

"Maybe so, but Islam is Allah's religion for the world. You and others like you are out of touch with reality because you do not treat religion as the dynamic it is in this struggle. We will win!"

"You will only succeed with collaborators."

"You are right. Their greed, their desire for power and political control is insatiable. By keeping the knowledge of political Islam confined to a few instead of making it available to everyone, its true danger is being nullified. The only way you will overcome us is by using all your resources, doing unpopular things, and attacking every aspect of the Islamic intrusion into your society. Right now, it doesn't look to me as if your government has the will and decisiveness to lead such an all-encompassing war. Our success in Europe bodes well for our efforts here."

"I understand the Brotherhood had an active military wing until things got out of control at Luxor in 1997, is that true?"

"Yes, a militant wing is not needed now that Al-Qaeda and other organizations are active, but it still exists. You know all it takes is a little coordination and you can have an operation as we attempted here. I would assume the Brotherhood will claim innocence and emphasize their nonviolent focus."

"If I were in the Brotherhood, it would just be logical for me to stir up trouble in Europe in the immigrant communities to gain more power. One thing for sure, the governments there are already in a dhimmi status. Don't you agree?"

"Yes."

"I certainly wouldn't call the riots and car burnings nonviolent and non-government instigated, would you?"

"I have nothing to offer on Europe."

"Well, how is your plan in the United States working? I have read it. In fact, I was the one that found your copy in Atlanta. That was a mistake, Mahmoud. It eventually led us to your doorstep."

Mahmoud hung his head and said, "It certainly was and it doesn't help my case with your government or my friends. But as to your question … our success has been outstanding. Your government is asleep. Muslims have infiltrated many governmental agencies and work silently like myself to impose Islam over your country. As I said, the very openness of your society and the freedoms you enjoy are working against you because there are those who do not realize you can only protect your freedoms by restricting some of those very freedoms when you are at war. Of course, the majority of your countrymen do not believe you are at war except in Afghanistan and Iraq. Yet the truth is, you are at war for the survival of your culture. Each day, we gain a little. The examples are many: Islamic teaching in the classrooms, a growing number of Islamic schools, more mosques, a political candidate here and there, the insertion of special religious demands in various places across the country, the firing of those speaking against the jihadist movement and dhimmitude in your country, apologist Middle East professors in your colleges, the Muslim Student Association on your campuses, and the use or nonuse of terms belie the true significance of our impact on your society. I could go on and on but these things are happening all around you, and you know I am right. All we have to do is continue in this same vein and your country will succumb. Mark my words."

This banter went on for another hour. Rick really did not learn much more about the Brotherhood. He still had a lot of research to do, but it had been interesting to hear these things from Mahmoud. Somehow, it made everything he'd read come alive, and it frightened the devil out of him. Mahmoud may have been captured this time but his seriousness and blind approach to his directions from Allah were very scary. His confidence in Allah, his contemporaries, and himself was amazing when you consider the task the Brotherhood has undertaken. Rick just did not know how he was going to convince the apathetic they were in very serious trouble. It sure was going to be one heck of a fight.

With those unhappy thoughts rambling through his brain, he thanked Mahmoud for talking to both George and him. He thanked George for his help and told him he'd have to mull over all he'd learned and do more research before putting anything on paper. Then, he called Ann for pick-up. It was close to five and he was weary.

When Ann arrived, she couldn't stop talking. It took everything he had to focus on her words. She'd seen two homes she'd really liked and wanted Rick to join her tomorrow to see them. He agreed. Trudy was excited because neither home was too far from them, and it would be wonderful to be so close. They went home to a quiet supper and evening. It had been a very different but rewarding day.

Chapter 28

Reunion

Sam and Trudy's hospitality was always exceptional. Their guests knew they were in the presence of special people. After they had all gathered at the table, Sam offered that this had been one of the most memorable weeks in his life, and he went on to say that it appeared to be the same for those around the table. He said it was strange how events could bring people together in unexpected ways and result in their being friends for life. He mentioned Rick, Ann, Mark, Ahmed, and Maria specifically. From this point on, they would always be the closest of friends and welcome in their home. Each was amazed how close they had become in such a short time and how meaningful they all were to one another.

Rick chimed in with his story of the week's events and ended by telling everyone he and Ann had found a house in Carrollwood and would be returning to Tampa in a couple of months. He wasn't sure exactly what his new job would be at the base nor was he sure they would want him after he published his article on the Brotherhood. He wasn't sure if his former editor would agree to publish it or if he would need to get another. Nevertheless, his article would be published. There was no question he would come to Tampa. Ann just listened with a smile on her face as she contemplated the group and their new home.

Najwa said she thought George ought to retire. He was just too old to be playing with the FBI in any capacity."

Abe offered, "You're right, Najwa. He is getting old. He's bald, flat-footed, beer-bellied, and getting slower all the time."

Everyone laughed.

"That isn't funny, Abe. A good Lebanese man is hard to find at any age and I have spent too many years training this one."

"Okay, Najwa, I was only kidding, but he is so good, it might be better to ask for a raise because I don't think Bud is going to want to change his assignment."

"Well, I am not going to give up trying. And I'd better not hear of any more adventures like the one this week …"

Cynthia poked Abe in the ribs and decided it would be better not to say any more about George, so he switched to Hannah, saying, "It is nice to see you and Mark are getting acquainted."

Hannah blushed but was obviously totally focused on Mark. She said simply, "We are enjoying one another's company, and the kids seem to be enjoying it too."

Mark was a little bolder, saying, "I'm on the road to ending my bachelorhood, the sooner the better. My parents fell in love in one evening, were married eight months later, and have fifty blissful years under their belt. I'm confident I've inherited their genes because my heart tells me Hannah is the girl of my dreams. I'm already committed and have begun the process of closing the deal before she changes her mind."

Everyone laughed as Hannah blushed, gave him a big hug, and said, "You're terrible!"

"I know, isn't it wonderful?"

With that, Ahmed commented, "Mark, you're right. The gal I loved got away and I've been wandering in the wilderness all these years without her. I'm just like you now, the sooner the better. I want to tie the knot before she gets away again. I believe I'd simply go nuts if something like that happened." Maria reacted much like Hannah.

Mark said, "Maybe we could do a double Lebanese wedding. You know, a spectacular with reporters and hundreds of people all crammed into the church."

With that, both women gasped in dismay. Hannah exclaimed, "Not on your life if you are talking about me!" Maria followed with a hearty, "NO!"

Everyone roared with laughter again.

Sam said, "Okay, you two, maybe I'd better have a talk with you. I'm not sure you understand how much trouble you're in already."

"Come on, Sam, I was only kidding on the double wedding. We'll enjoy attending each other's when the time comes," said Mark.

"That's right, you'd better pull your horns in quickly, but I'm not sure you are out of trouble yet."

Hannah said, "It's obvious these two need some training. Maria and I will have to give all this some more thought."

Sam sighed, "We are so blessed to have each of you as friends and that will never change, but I need to let you know I have accepted a new job. It will probably take me out of town a little more often than in the past. I'll be acting as a marketing representative for a defense contractor selling equipment and training devices in the Middle East. I've been kind of restless these past six months, and this will give me an opportunity to visit some old friends and haunts around the Mediterranean. It will be fun, and Trudy will be able to accompany me on many of my trips. Tampa will remain our home base. We'll just be on the road a bit more."

Rick piped up, "Holy cow, at your age that sounds pretty challenging. Woops … sorry, Trudy … I was talking about that guy you run around with all the time." Everyone laughed again.

"Well, Rick, you just have to understand you can't keep an old warrior corralled. If you try it, you might break their heart, and that would be worse than following them around the world," admonished Trudy.

"Okay, okay … I was only kidding. I not only know you are right, I suppose I'll be doing the same thing some day."

"I don't doubt it at all, Rick. You and Ann have the same adventuresome spirit."

George interrupted, saying, "More power to you, Sam. We are behind you 100 percent … right, Najwa?"

Everyone took the clue and said, "Right."

George laughed, "You see, Najwa, if work is good enough for Sam, I'm sure you would agree my work with the FBI falls into the same category … don't you?"

"Wait until I get you home, George Ayoub … I have a few things to bring to your attention." Laughter again.

With that, Ahmed decided it was time to announce his baptism in the morning at Abe's church. He explained it had been a long time since Maria led him to Christ in that small village in southern Lebanon. He told them of how over the years he would secretly read the Bible, listen to Christian TV, and sneak into churches whenever the opportunity presented itself. The conflict between his inner self and the public life he lived as a Muslim was constantly present and often tore at his determination. Yet, he knew he was doing the right thing because the Lord provided peace and joy in his heart at the same time. The most painful part was not being able to talk to anyone about Christ, particularly his beloved Maria. He knew in his heart that any such conversations would open wounds that might lead him to acknowledge Christ publicly and end his usefulness in fighting the jihadists in the most effective way he knew. He acknowledged that he did not deserve the miracle the Lord had provided in putting the two of them together again, but he was convinced it was manifold evidence of the Lord's grace and great love for them both that had brought it about. Call it what you will, he knew beyond a shadow of doubt that his Lord loved him and would stand with them as he had over the years, while each had led such different lives, only to be brought together again in this manner. He said he was overwhelmed with joy and his public confession of faith tomorrow would be the most wonderful day in his life next to that of marrying Maria. He asked that not only his family but also all his newfound friends be present on this wonderful occasion to stand with him.

Thinking of the years of sacrifice he had assumed to do what the Lord had placed upon his heart and the miracle of the recent reunion, more than a few tears appeared among those who would stand with him in the morning, and all agreed they would be present.

As the evening ended and the good-byes were exchanged, they realized in one way or another, the morning would bring new adventures for all of them.

ACKNOWLEDGMENTS

This novel came to life because of a strong desire to help educate others as to the true meanings underlying the doctrinal aspects of Islam set forth by Mohammad in the Koran and by others in the Hadith and Sira (biography) of Mohammad. The doctrinal conflicts in these texts are difficult for the average Westerner to comprehend without someone to interpret them. Sometimes, they are even difficult for the most serious scholar to unravel. Nevertheless, Westerners must confront them if they are to avoid being deceived by those who mean us harm.

I have studied and taught these subjects, so the natural follow-on seemed to be a book, not an academic text, but a novel that would contain the doctrinal truths of political Islam and be written in such a manner as to touch a wider audience. Regardless, it wasn't until I read the publications of the Center for the Study of Political Islam that I was inspired to set pen to paper. The result was *Out of Darkness*.

It was CSPI's analysis that made the essence of Islamic doctrine come alive to me because it was clear, realistic, and easy to understand. At the same time, the Center approached political Islam from a non-Muslim's perspective. Therefore, their work is not neutral. Their focus was strictly on Mohammad and doctrine, staying clear of general discussions of Muslims in today's society.

As you would expect, there is one overall doctrine in Islam. It addresses all the political, cultural, and religious aspects of the faith. Unfortunately, most people think of Islam as a religion and do not consider its political aspects; therefore, most writers talk in terms of the Koran and Hadith but do not add the Sira (the biography of Mohammad) in their analysis. The Center for the Study of Political Islam considers all three documents to be the texts defining Islamic doctrine and refers to them as the "Trilogy of Islam." Their publications detail the dualistic nature of the doctrine along with the dualistic ethics and dualistic logic it encompasses. Indeed, the Center's major intellectual breakthrough was seeing that dualism is the foundation and key to understanding Islam. This is a refreshing approach that assists the reader in coming to terms with the most critical aspects of the religion while clarifying the true significance of the doctrine. I have not found other publications setting forth the doctrine in such a simple, clear, and concise manner. Because of this, I have made liberal use of the Center's material. Naturally, the nature of the novel and the dialogue between individuals does not easily lend itself to footnoting of adapted material. As a result, I wish to acknowledge the cutting-edge nature of the Center's publications, the academic excellence they represent, and their use throughout the discussions concerning the truth about political Islam. Mr. Bill Warner, the Center's editor, met with my wife and I to discuss my endeavors; he encouraged the use of the Center's material and reviewed the manuscript. His efforts inspired rewrites and the determination to continue with the project. I am truly grateful for his thoughtful support.

Another work I would like to acknowledge is Bruce Bickel and Stan Jantz's *Bruce & Stan's Pocket Guide to Islam*. This small but packed quick reference book encapsulates and simplifies many of the teachings of Islam as compared to Christianity; particularly worthwhile to this novel were the discussions on the powers of Allah, Muslims' knowledge of Allah, Jesus in Islam, original sin, and salvation. Additionally, outstanding books are listed in the Bibliography should you be interested in pursuing this subject further in greater depth. I would encourage you to do so.

Lastly, this work would never have reached fruition without the love and support of my wife, my family members, and a myriad of faithful friends who encouraged me in every respect. Many read the manuscript and offered helpful suggestions to enhance the story line. In all cases, encouragement accompanied their suggestions and lifted my spirits as I went through the publication process. Many, many thanks to all!

NOTES

In many cases, the footnotes include the actual text from which a conversational concept was developed in the novel. This is unusual but the author thought it important because the actual conversation in the novel didn't necessarily lend itself to a verbatim quote. Then too the notes often provide additional information of interest. In all instances it is believed these notes add to the readers understanding of Islamic doctrines.

Chapter 3

1. Schanzer, Jonathan, "Middle East Studies on the Mend," The American Thinker, January 4, 2009.
2. Scarborough, Rowan, CAIR Trains FBI Agents as New Report Cites Links to Terror, www.insight-report.com, March 18–24.

Chapter 5

1. The author considers the terms "Mecca Muslim(s)," meaning a more peaceful doctrinal approach, and "Medina Muslim(s)," meaning a more violent doctrinal approach, more doctrinally definitive than current media uses of "moderate" and "radical." The media terms are Westernized and tend to obviate the true Islamic doctrines set forth in Mecca and Medina.

2. Akram, Mohamed, An Explanatory Memorandum on the General Strategic Goal for the Group in North America, May 22, 1991, pp. 2–18. The Arabic words Ikhwan and mujahedeen have an English translation in parenthesis.

Chapter 6

1. Center for the Study of Political Islam (CSPI), "Mohammad and the Unbelievers," in The Islamic Trilogy, Vol. 1, p. vii and "The Political Traditions of Mohammad," in Vol. 2, p. vii, and Ali, Abdullah Yusef, Qur'an, Tahrike Tarsile Qur'an, Elmhurst, NY, Sura 5:3 and 5:101.
2. Ibid., p. vii.
3. Ibid., p. 168. "Islam is not the worship of Allah. Islam is the worship of Allah by imitating Mohammad." And p. viii–ix. "Muslims believe that Mohammad's attitude, actions, and words are the ideal pattern of human behavior for all times and all peoples. The smallest detail of his life teaches pure Islam. It is for that reason that each chapter starts with a verse from the Koran that commands all Muslims to imitate Mohammad in every detail of his words and deeds. Mohammad's life defines Islam."

Chapter 7

1. The Center for the Study of Political Islam is the first to use the term "Trilogy." The author has not encountered it previously, principally because most writers only discuss the Koran and Hadith. More often or not, the Sira is left out of their discussions.
2. CSPI, The Islamic Trilogy, Vol. 2, p. viii, "The Trilogy is the foundation and totality of Islam. Every one of the hundreds of biographies of Mohammad is based upon the Sira and Hadith. All of Islamic law, the Shari'a, is based upon the Trilogy. Every statement and action of political or religious Islam comes from the Trilogy, including the events of September 11, 2001. If you are familiar with the Trilogy, you can talk with an Islamic religious and political leader

or critique an article written in a scholarly journal such as Foreign Affairs. Once you know the Trilogy, you will see every news report about Islam with new eyes."

3. Ibid., Vol. 2, p. 163. Islam does not simply say Allah is the One-God. Why? Without Mohammad there is no Islam. To worship Allah, the One-God, does not make you a Muslim. Humanity must worship Allah exactly as Mohammad did. Only worshipping the One-God, Allah, the way Mohammad did can make you a Muslim. It takes Allah and Mohammad to make Islam. A Muslim must be a Mohammadan. (Note: a Mohammadan no more worships Mohammad than a Confucian worships Confucius.) The non-Muslim has no need for concern about Paradise and Hell of Allah. What is of concern is how a secularist, a Christian, a Hindu, a Jew, or any other non-Muslim will be treated today, not after death.

4. CSPI, The Islamic Trilogy, Vol. 1, p. 168.

Chapter 9

1. Glaszov, Jamie, The Study of Political Islam, Frontpagemagazine.com, February 5, 2007. Interview with Mr. Bill Warner, CSPI, "All of our politics and ethics are based upon a unitary ethic that is best formulated in the Golden Rule: Treat others as you would be treated … everyone wants to be treated as a human being … we all want to be equal under the law and be treated as social equals. On the basis of the Golden Rule—the equality of human beings—we have created democracy, ended slavery, and treat women and men as political equals … All religions have some version of the Golden Rule except Islam."

2. CSPI, The Islamic Trilogy, An Abridged Koran, Vol. IV, p. 199, "The ethical system of the Koran is also dualistic. How a person is treated depends upon his being a believer or an unbeliever. There is one set of ethics for the believer and another set of ethics for the unbeliever. Deceit, violence, and force are acceptable against the unbelievers who resist

the logic of the Koran. Believers are to be treated as brothers and sisters. Good is what advances Islam. Evil is whatever resists Islam. Vol. 1, p. 163, "Duality of ethics was the basis for Mohammad's greatest single invention—Jihad. Jihad is dual ethics with sacred violence. The key religious element of the dual ethics is that Allah sanctifies violence for complete domination. The non-Muslims must submit to Islam."

3. Glaszov, Jamie, Warner Interview, February 5, 2007, p. 3, "The term 'human being' has no meaning inside of Islam. There is no such thing as humanity, only duality of the believer and unbeliever. Look at the ethical statements found in the Hadith. A Muslim should not lie, cheat, kill or steal from other Muslims. But a Muslim may lie, deceive or kill an unbeliever if it advances Islam. There is no such thing as a universal statement of ethics in Islam. Muslims are to be treated one way and unbelievers another way. The closest Islam comes to a universal statement of ethics is that the entire world must submit to Islam."

4. Ibid., p. 3, "All of science is based upon the law of contradiction. If two things contradict each other, then at least one of them has to be false. But inside of Islamic logic, two contradictory statements can both be true. Islam uses dualistic logic and we use unitary logic."

5. Ibid., p. 2, "Dualistic systems can only be measured by statistics … Let's turn to Bukhari [the Hadith] for the answer, as he repeatedly speaks of Jihad. In Bukhari 97 percent of the jihad references are about war and 3 percent are about the inner struggle. So the statistical answer is that jihad is 97 percent war and 3 percent inner struggle. Is jihad war? Yes—97 percent. Is jihad inner struggle? Yes—3 percent.

6. CSPI, The Islamic Trilogy, Vol. 1, p. 164 and CSPI, A Christian's Self-Study Course on Islam, "Three Levels of Learning, Levels 2 & 3," pp. 3–85, "The Koran is very clear about jihad. All the jihad verses abrogate the 'good' Meccan verses. The 'good' verses are used by those Muslims who are

too weak to do jihad. When immigrants first arrive in the host country (Islam's terms for kafir lands), they talk about peace and brotherhood, while making demands about civil rights. As Islam grows in strength the demands increase in scope. As an example: Kafir laws should not apply to Islamic families, only Islamic law will do. All jihad can be divided into pressure and violence. The first forms of violence are crime and riots. An Islamic riot is a battle in a civil war. These are taking place now in Europe. Europeans, who are as ignorant as American Kafirs, see them as civil rights demonstrations, not jihad."

7. Glaszov, Jamie, Warner Interview, p. 3, "Since Islam has a dualistic logic and dualistic ethics, it is completely foreign to us. Muslims think differently from us and feel differently from us. So our aversion is based upon fear and a rejection of Islamic ethics and logic. This aversion causes us to avoid learning about Islam so we are ignorant and stay ignorant."

8. Ibid., p. 3, "Another part of the aversion is the realization that there is no compromise with dualistic ethics. There is no halfway place between unitary ethics and dualistic ethics … in short, Islamic politics, ethics, and logic cannot be part of our civilization. Islam does not assimilate, it dominates." And p. 5, "Political Islam has annihilated every culture it has invaded or immigrated to. The total time for annihilation takes centuries, but once Islam is ascendant it never fails. The host culture disappears and become extinct. We must learn the doctrine of political Islam to survive. The doctrine is very clear that all forms of force and persuasion may and must be used to conquer us."

9. Ibid., p. 5, "Christians believe that 'love conquers all.' Well, love does not conquer Islam. Christians have a difficult time seeing Islam as a political doctrine, not a religion." CSPI, A Christian's Self-Study Course on Islam, pp. 2–16, "While there are over 300 references in the Koran to Allah and fear, there are 49 references to love. Of these references,

227

39 are negative such as the 14 negative references to love of money, power, other gods and status. Three verses command humanity to love Allah and 2 verses tell about how Allah loves the believer. There are 25 verses about how Allah does not love kafirs. This leaves 5 verses about love. Of these 5, 3 are about loving kin or a Muslim brother. One verse commands a Muslim to give for the love of Allah. This leaves only one quasi-universal verse about love: give what you love to charity and even this is contaminated by dualism since Muslim charity only goes to other Muslims. There is not a verse about either compassion or love of a kafir, but there are 14 verses that teach that a Muslim is not a friend of a kafir. Islamic Hell is primarily political. Hell is mentioned 146 times in the Koran. Only 9 references are for moral failings—greed, lack of charity, or love of worldly success. The other 137 references to Hell involve eternal torture for disagreeing with Mohammad. Thus 94 percent of the references to Hell are as a political prison for dissenters."

Chapter 10

1. CSPI, A Christian's Self-Study Course on Islam, pp. 2-13 to 2-14, "The Trilogy is the foundation of Islam. All biographies of Mohammad are based upon the Sira and Hadith. All of Islamic law, the Shari'a, is based upon the Trilogy. Every statement and action of political and religious Islam come from the Trilogy. The Koran is compared wrongly to the Bible. The Koran is only 14 percent of Islam's sacred texts and does not contain nearly enough information to tell someone how to be a Muslim. The Muslim Bible would be the Koran, the Sira and the Hadith. The Koran is similar to the Torah, the first five books of the Old Testament. The Sira compares to the Gospels and the Hadith has similarities to the Letters. Measured by the textual doctrine, Islam is 86 percent Mohammad and 14 percent Allah. But since Mohammad is the only person whoever 'heard' from Allah,

the Koran is really about Mohammad. So Islam is 100 percent Mohammad."

2. Ali, Abdullah Yusef, Qur'an, Sira 5:101, Tahrike Tarsile Qur'an, Inc., Elmhurst, NY, p. 74, "O you who believe! Do not ask questions about things which if made plain to you may cause you trouble. But if you ask about things when the Qur'an is being revealed, they will be made plain to you, Allah will forgive those: for Allah is Oft-forgiving, Most Forbearing." Morey, Robert, The Islamic Invasion, Confronting the World's Fastest Growing Religion, Christian Scholars Press, Las Vegas, NV, pp. 157–158, "While the devout Muslim believes with all of his heart that the rituals and doctrines of Islam are entirely heavenly in origin and thus cannot have any earthly sources, Middle East scholars have demonstrated beyond all doubt the every ritual and belief in Islam can be traced back to pre-Islamic Arabian culture. In other words, Mohammad did not preach anything new. Everything he taught had been believed and practiced in Arabia long before he was ever born. Even the idea of 'only one God' was borrowed from the Jews and the Christians. This irrefutable fact casts to the ground the Muslim claim that Islam was revealed from heaven. Since its rituals, beliefs, and even the Qur'an itself can be fully explained in terms of pre-Islamic sources in Arabian culture, this means that the religion of Islam is false. It is no surprise, therefore, the Western scholars have concluded that Allah is not God, Mohammad was not his prophet, and the Qur'an is not the Word of God."

Chapter 11

1. The dialogue about kafir is taken from two sources:

   a. CSPI, A Christian's Self-Study Course on Islam, 2-59, "Kafir defines the ethical dualism at a personal level. To call someone a kafir is an ethical statement. A Muslim may be friendly to a kafir if it advances Islam, but he is not actually a friend. A kafir is not a real human; Muslims are the only real humans. The only good in a kafir is how far the kafir can serve to enrich Islam.

b. CSPI, Thirteen Lessons on Political Islam, Islam 101, 2008, p. 15, "Most of the Koran is about non-Muslims. It has special names for all the different types of people who don't believe Mohammad. One of these names that the Koran uses is kafir. This word is usually translated as unbeliever, but this is wrong. One of the greatest failings of non-Muslims is their use of language to describe Islam. The words that non-Muslims use don't show a real understanding of Islamic doctrine. Take for example the word unbeliever. Unbeliever is logically correct, but the problem is that it does not go far enough. Unbeliever is emotionally neutral. Kafir is negatively charged to a degree that has no equal in English."

2. CSPI, A Christian's Self-Study Course on Islam, p. 3-52, "After taking the property of Jews as the spoils of war, the Muslims made an agreement called a dhimma with the Jews in Arabia. The Jews could stay and farm the land if they gave Islam half their profits. They then became dhimmis who were under the protection of Islam. Thus the word dhimmi came to mean permanent, second-class kafir citizens in a country ruled by Islam. Dhimmis paid a special tax, and their civil and legal rights were greatly limited. The only way out of being a dhimmi was to convert to Islam or flee. The taxes from the dhimmis made Islam rich. There are very few Hadiths about dhimmitude, but it was another of Mohammad's unique political inventions. The scorched-earth policy of killing all nonbelievers was satisfying to the warrior, but it had an inherent problem: once everyone was killed, the warrior had to find other work. Mohammad therefore created the policy of dhimmitude to deal with the Jews. Dhimmitude was expanded later to include Christians, Magians, and others.

3. Ibid., p. 3-52, "It can be argued that the glory of Islam came not from Islam but its dhimmis' wealth and knowledge.... The dhimmis were the scholars, since the Arabs of Mohammad's day were barely literate and their classical literature was oral poetry," and p. 3-53, "From carpets to architecture, the Muslims took the ideas of the dhimmis and obtained historical credit."

4. Ibid., p. 3-55.

Chapter 12

1. Bickel, Bruce and Jantz, Stan, Bruce & Stan's Pocket Guide to Islam, Harvest House, Eugene, OR, 2002, p. 34.

2. Ibid., pp. 38–39.

3. Ibid, pp. 35–37; CSPI, A Christian's Self-Study Course on Islam, p. 2-16; Caner, Ergun Mehmet and Caner, Emir Fethi, Unveiling Islam, An Insider's Look at Muslim Life and Beliefs, Kregel Publications, Grand Rapids, MI, 2002, p. 30, "GOD LOVES YOU! This is the brash claim of Christianity. The key, in fact, to winning people to a saving faith in Jesus Christ as Savior is based upon this claim. Yet in the Qur'an, no such statement is to be found. Whereas the Bible teaches that God hates sin and is angry with sinners (e.g., Prov. 6:16–19, Jer. 4:4, Rom. 1:18, and James 4:4), Islamic scripture affirms that Allah hates sinners: 'For Allah loves not transgressors.' (Surah 2:190)." Ibid., p. 118, "Islam also looks to a god of the scales, as opposed to the atoning God the Son. Allah forgives only at the repentance of the Muslim, and all consequences for sin and debt of guilt fall on the Muslim, who comes to Allah in terror, hoping for a commutation of his sentence. Allah is a 'Liberal Giver' (Al-Wahab), but with the character of a fierce warrior who decides to be merciful in response to victory. Again, one sees a judge, as opposed to a God of love."

4. CSPI, A Christian Self-Study Course on Islam, p. 2-16. This summarizes the text pertaining to love and the Koran. The entire section is quoted in Note 10 for Chapter 9.

5. CSPI, The Islamic Trilogy, Vol. IV, p. 198, "The highest form of living is to die for Allah in Jihad. Death, Paradise, and Hell are the values of Islam. The proper relationship between Allah and humanity is master/slave (Muslims are the slaves of Allah) and fear (there are over 300 references to the fear of Allah, the Merciful)."

6. CSPI, A Christian Self-Study Course on Islam, p. 2-39, "Muslims say that Christians, Jews, and Muslims are all part of the 'Abrahamic faith.' It is not part of the Meccan Koran that 'proves' Islam is true as being an extension of Judaism. The only way a Christian is actually a Christian, according to Islam, is that if the Christian says that Mohammad is the final prophet of God, Christ was a Muslim prophet, the New Testament is corrupt, and there is no Trinity. Only those Christians who admit this are members of the Abrahamic faith. All other Christians are not Christians, but infidels or kafirs." CSPI, The Islamic Trilogy, Vol. 1, p. 7, "Mecca was a long way from Syria where Abraham dwelt, but the Meccans claimed Abraham and Ishmael had built the Kabah in ancient times."

7. Ibid., pp. 2-39, 3-107, and 3-108, "Not a single person in Mohammad's Mecca is named Abraham, Ishmael, or Hagar. Not one. Why? They had no knowledge about any relationship between Arabs and Abraham. They knew of the Jews and Abraham, but they made no claim of kinship with their names. After Mohammad, these names became common amongst Muslims." CSPI, A Christian Self-Study Course on Islam, pp. 2-39, 3-47, "Islam asserted that Christians had hidden the prophesies that said Mohammad would come to fulfill the work of Christ. To believe in the divinity of Christ is to refuse to submit to Islam. Those Christians who believe in the divinity of Christ and refuse to submit to Islam are kafirs and infidels. Like the Jews, only those Christians who submit to Islam, become dhimmis and are ruled by Shari'a (Islamic law) are actual Christians. Islam defines all religions and only Islam can talk about

Islam.… Under Islam, Christians can revere Jesus, but they must accept Mohammad as the final prophet. He is superior to Jesus. The New and Old Testaments must be seen as corrupted and weak. Any conflict between the Koran and Bible is because the Bible is wrong. The Koran is absolutely perfect and the Bible was changed to cover up its prophecies of Mohammad. Jesus must be more important than Noah. This is the Christianity accepted by Islam. This is what Islam calls the 'real' Christianity. Islam sees all forms of Christianity as profoundly wrong. Tragically, today we find deluded Christians who say, 'Christians and Muslims worship the same god. We are both members of the Abrahamic faith.' This is based upon a profound ignorance."

Chapter 13

1. Bickel, Bruce and Jantz, Stan, Bruce & Stan's Pocket Guide to Islam, pp. 39–41 and 70–73.
2. CSPI, The Islamic Trilogy, Vol. 1, p. 56. "While the Christians were in Medina, they argued religion with Mohammad. They held forth with the doctrine of the Trinity—God, Christ, and the Holy Spirit—and the divinity of Christ. Mohammad later laid out the Islamic doctrine of Christ." (Ed.: The Koran regards the Trinity of the Christians to be Allah, Jesus, and Mary.)
3. CSPI, The Islamic Trilogy, Vol. 1, p. x, "Ishaq's Sira contains many stories of miracles; yet it also says Mohammad refused to perform miracles. The Koran's text is older than the Sira and says that Mohammad was a messenger who did no miracles." Ibid., p. 51, "A running commentary of the Sira claims that the Jews and Christians corrupted their sacred texts in order to conceal the fact that the coming of Mohammad was prophesied in their scriptures. The stories in the Koran are similar to those of the Jewish scriptures, but they have different plots and make different points. According to Islam the difference is that the real Torah (the first five books of the Jewish scriptures: Genesis, Exodus,

Leviticus, Numbers, and Deuteronomy) is in the Koran. Mohammad said the scriptures of the Jews were changed to hide the fact that Islam is the true religion. According to him, the Jewish scriptures are corrupt; the Koran is perfect and contains real stories."

4. CSPI, A Christian Self-Study Course on Islam, p. 3-82, "The story of the Koran culminates in the dominance of political Islam. The Koran teaches that Islam is the perfect political system and is destined to rule the entire world. The governments and constitutions of the world must all submit to political Islam. If the political systems of the kafirs do not submit, then force, jihad may be used. All jihad is defensive, since refusing to submit to Islam is an offense against Allah. All Muslims must support the political action of jihad. This may take several forms—fighting, proselytizing or contributing money."

5. Virtually all of the pagan rituals of Arabia Moon god worship were incorporated into Islam, particularly the Hajj. CSPI, The Islamic Trilogy, Vol. 1, p. 2, "The legend about the Kabah in Mecca was that Abraham, the patriarch of the Jews, had built it. The Kabah was used for religious rituals and served as a community center. Rituals established by Qusayy included prostrations (bowing down to the earth), ritual prayers, circling the Kabah while praying, and drinking from the well called Zam Zam. Other rituals included throwing stones at pillars that symbolized the devil."

Chapter 15

1. Bickel, Bruce and Jantz, Stan, Bruce & Stan's Pocket Guide to Islam, pp. 88–90. "It is important to remember that for the Muslim, everything begins with Allah. Islam means 'submission,' and the Muslim is one who submits to Allah and obeys him. The greatest sin in Islam is idolatry, or shirk, which is giving to anybody or anything even a tiny piece of Allah's unique sovereignty. So how does Islam view the origin of sin? The Qur'an describes the Fall in much the

same way the Bible does: Adam and Eve were created and placed in a beautiful garden and were allowed to eat any fruit they wanted except the fruit of one tree they could not touch (Surah 2:35). Satan tempted Adam and Eve, and they sinned. Their rebellion against Allah and his holy will had a devastating effect on the entire human race. All people were affected by the fall. Muslims believe that man has a moral weakness rather than a sinful nature. He was kicked out of the Garden, but man is not separated from God. According to Abdiyah Akbar Abdul-Haqq, some Islamic traditions teach that a child is born 'naturally inclined toward a true religion, which is understood to be Islam.' In other words, every child is born a Muslim naturally, but is perverted after birth by his environment. Mohammad is reported to have said that every infant is born 'on God's plan,' but then his parents make him a Jew or Christian."

2. Ibid., pp. 92–93, "Islam also reaches salvation by faith, but with one added feature: good deeds. Despite their unwavering belief in the sovereignty of Allah and his ability to save, Muslims believe in the necessity of contributing to the salvation process with works, but not just any works. To a Muslim, good deeds must be compatible with the teaching of the Qur'an and Hadith. Like Christianity, Islam views sin as a debt. But rather than asking God to forgive the debt by faith in Jesus Christ, Islam teaches that people must 'discharge the debt' by doing good. Allah forgives sins, but there are conditions that must be met. This is why the five pillars of faith are so important in Islam. The Muslim must practice these duties in order to gain paradise."

3. See Note 7 for Chapter 9 and CSPI, A Christian Self-Study Course on Islam, p. 3-112.

4. CSPI, The Islamic Trilogy, Vol. 2, p. 67, "Humiliation and contempt were an important part of the ethic in relating to Jews. The favorite epitaph for a Jew was the one Mohammad used, 'apes.' Christians were called 'pigs.' Dhimmis were never to have higher status than Muslims."

5. CSPI, A Christian Self-Study Course on Islam, p. 3-102.
6. CSPI, A Christian Self-Study Course on Islam, p. 3-102 and various single statements highlighting different CSPI teaching points.

BIBLIOGRAPHY

Al-Misri, Ahmad ibn Naqib, *Reliance of the Traveller: A Classic Manual of Islamic Sacred Law* (In Arabic with facing English Text, Commentary, and Appendices Edited and Translated by Nuh Ha Min Keller), Amana, Beltsville, MD, 1994.

Anderson, Kirby, *A Biblical Point of View on Islam*, Harvest House, Eugene, OR, 2008.

Anonymous, *Imperial Hubris: Why the West Is Losing the War on Terror*, Brassey's, Washington, D.C., 2004.

Babbin, Jed, *Inside the Asylum: Why the United Nations and Old Europe Are Worse than You Think*, Regency. Washington, D.C., 2004.

Baer, Robert, *Sleeping with the Devil: How Washington Sold Our Soul for Saudi Crude*, Three Rivers Press, New York, 2003.

Bayat, Asef, *Making Islam Democratic, Social Movements and the Post-Islamist Turn*. Stanford University Press, Stanford, CA, 2007.

Benard, Cheryl, *Civil Democratic Islam: Partners, Resources, and Strategies*, Rand National Security Research Division, Arlington, VA, 2003.

Benard, Cheryl; Rabasa, Angel; Schwartz, Lowell H.; and Sickle, Peter, *Building Moderate Muslim Networks*, Rand Corporation, Santa Monica, CA, 2007.

Bickel, Bruce and Jantz, Stan, *Bruce & Stan's Pocket Guide to Islam*, Harvest House, Eugene, OR, 2002.

Blankley, Tony, *The West's Last Chance: Will We Win the Clash of Civilizations?* Regency, Washington, D.C., 2005.

Canter, Ergun Mehmet (General Editor), *Voices Behind the Veil: The World of Islam Through the Eyes of Women*, Kregel, Grand Rapids, MI, 2003.

Center for the Study of Political Islam (CSPI), *A Christian's Self-Study Course on Islam, Three Levels of Learning, Levels 2 & 3*, CSPI, USA, 2008.

Center for the Study of Political Islam (CSPI). *The Islamic Trilogy, Mohammad and the Unbelievers, A Political Life*, Vol. 1, CSPI, USA, 2006.

Center for the Study of Political Islam (CSPI). *The Islamic Trilogy: The Political Traditions of Mohammed, The Hadith for the Unbelievers*, Vol. 2, CSPI, USA, 2006.

Center for the Study of Political Islam (CSPI). *The Islamic Trilogy: A Simple Koran, Readable and Understandable*, Vol. 3, CSPI, USA, 2006.

Center for the Study of Political Islam (CSPI). *The Islamic Trilogy: An Abridged Koran, Readable and Understandable*, Vol. 4, CSPI, USA, 2006.

Center for the Study of Political Islam (CSPI), *Thirteen Lessons on Political Islam, Islam 101*, CSPI, USA, 2008.

Delong-Bas, Natana J., *Wahhabi Islam: From Revival and Reform to Global Jihad*, Oxford University Press, New York, 2004.

Demy, Timothy and Stewart, Gary P., *In the Name of God: Understanding the Mindset of Terrorism*, Harvest House, Eugene, OR, 2002.

Fallaci, Oriana, *The Force of Reason*, Rizzoli International, New York, 2006.

Freedom House, Center for Religious Freedom, *Saudi Publications on Hate Ideology Fill American Mosques*, Washington, D. C., 2005.

Friedman, Thomas L., *The World Is Flat: A Brief History of the Twenty-First Century*, Farrar, Straus, & Giroux, New York, 2005.

Gabriel, Brigitte, *Because They Hate: A Survivor of Islamic Terror Warns America*, St. Martin's Press, New York, 2006.

Gabriel, Brigitte, *They Must Be Stopped: Why We Must Defeat Radical Islam and How We Can Do It*, St. Martin's Press, New York, 2008.

Guillaume, A. *The Life of Mohammad: A Translation of Ibn Ishaq's Sirat Rasul Allah*, Oxford University Press, Karachi, Pakistan, 1967.

Hart, Benjamin, *Radical Islam vs. America*, Green Hill, Ottawa, IL, 2003.

Huntington, Samuel P., *Clash of Civilizations*, Touchstone, New York, New York, 1996.

Ibn Warraq, *Why I Am Not a Muslim*, Prometheus, Amherst, NY, 1995.

Ibrahim, Raymond, *The Al-Qaeda Reader*, Broadway Books, New York, 2007.

Lawrence, Bruce (Editor) and Howarth, James (Translator), *Messages to the World: The Statements of Osama Bin Laden*, VERSO, London and New York, 2005.

Manji, Irshad, *The Trouble with Islam Today: A Muslim's Call for Reform in Her Faith*, St. Martin's Griffin, New York.

Morey, Robert A., *The Islamic Invasion: Confronting the World's Fastest Growing Religion*, Christian Scholars Press, Las Vegas, NV, 1992.

Parshall, Phil, *Understanding Muslim Teachings and Traditions: A Guide for Christians*, Baker Books, Grand Rapids, MI, 1994.

Phillips, Melanie, *Londonstan*, Encounter Books, New York, 2006.

Qutb, Sayyid, *Milestones* (Revised Translation), American Trust, Indianapolis, 1990.

Richardson, Don, *Secrets of the Koran: Revealing Insights into Islam's Holy Book*, Regal, Ventura, CA, 2003.

Spencer, Robert, *Stealth Jihad: How Radical Islam Is Subverting America without Guns or Bombs*, Regency, Washington, D.C.

Sperry, Paul, *Infiltration: How Muslim Spies and Subversives Have Penetrated Washington*, Nelson Current, Nashville, TN, 2005.

Trofimov, Yaroslav, *Faith at War: A Journey on the Frontlines of Islam, From Baghdad to Timbuktu*, Henry Holt, New York, 2005.

Wagner, William, Dr., *How Islam Plans to Change the World*, Kregel, Grand Rapids, MI, 2004.

Williams, Paul L., *Osama's Revenge: The Next 9/11, What the Media and the Government Haven't Told You*, Prometheus, Amherst, New York, 2004.

Ye'or, Bat, *Eurabia: The Euro-Arab Axis*, Associated University Presses, Cranbury, NJ, 2005.

Zacharias, Ravi, *Light in the Shadow of Jihad: The Struggle for Truth*, Multnomah, Sisters, OR, 2002.

LaVergne, TN USA
15 December 2009
167089LV00003B/7/P